100 COMPLETELY
NEW IDEAS
FOR MANAGING BEHAVIOUR

100 COMPLETELY NEW IDEAS
FOR MANAGING BEHAVIOUR

Johnnie Young

CONTINUUM ONE HUNDREDS

continuum

Continuum International Publishing Group

The Tower Building
11 York Road
London, SE1 7NX

80 Maiden Lane
Suite 704
New York, NY 10038

www.continuumbooks.com

British Library Cataloguing-in-Publication Data
A catalogue record for this book is available from the British Library.

ISBN: 978-1-4411-6908-2 (paperback)

Library of Congress Cataloging-in-Publication Data
A catalog record for this book is available from the Library of Congress.

Typeset by Newgen Imaging Systems Pvt Ltd, Chennai, India
Printed and bound in India

This book is dedicated, as always,
to my wife Sylvie and my three children
Edward, Julie and William.

CONTENTS

SECTION 3   It's Not What You Teach, It's How You Teach It

SECTION 4   The Language and Attitude of Success

SECTION 5 **For Immediate Effect**

SECTION 6 **Building Longer Term Strategies**

SECTION 7 **Common Dangers and How to Avoid Them**

SECTION 8 **Getting to the Heart of Problems through Role Plays**

SECTION 9 **Dealing with Extreme Behaviours**

SECTION 10 **A Few 'Off The Wall' Strategies**

ACKNOWLEDGEMENTS

I would like to thank my publishers, Continuum, and in particular Melanie Wilson for all her help and professionalism.

I would also like to thank all the teachers, experienced and new, who have attended my Behaviour Management Training sessions over the years. The positive comments you have made are greatly appreciated.

I would like to thank the staff I work with at Clacton Coastal Academy. You are a wonderful team of people, I love working with you and I continue to learn so much from you. It is extremely difficult to single out individuals but I would like to mention in particular, Richard Battye, Anthony Davenport, Dianne Bignell and Katy Middleditch. Your friendship and support over the years means more than I can say.

There is one last mention. Teachers need someone who is not a teacher to give them a sense of reality and to stop them becoming consumed by the profession. I would like to thank Paul Welham, my lifelong friend, for just being there.

Dealing effectively with the behaviour of students is a huge part of a teacher's job and requires great skill and experience. When I started out teaching nearly two decades ago, I nearly gave it all up because I thought I wasn't cut out to be a teacher. Then I realized that nobody is cut out to be a teacher. You have to learn the craft. By watching and learning from others, by making notes and by experimenting with the best practice I was able to gradually become better at behaviour management.

I now teach new and experienced teachers and I have published *100 Ideas for Managing Behaviour* and *100+ Ideas for Managing Behaviour*. I still don't find it easy. Every lesson is a challenge. But what I love is that, the more skill you have, the more enjoyable the challenge becomes and the reward is to see better behaviour which leads to better learning from your students.

These new ideas are based on the ideas I have used, in addition to ones in my books already published, and those that I have taught in my training sessions. It is the feedback from these sessions which has drawn my attention to the techniques which the participants have found to be really useful and effective.

In Section 1, I have tried to distil the most important core skills. In Section 2, I have included some ideas where the focus is on planning and systems which are designed to prevent trouble happening, rather than dealing with it once it has happened. Section 3 looks more closely at examples of how the work itself can be delivered in a way to enhance behaviour management. Section 4 aims to show how the power of positive language will be of enormous help in the managing of behaviour. Section 5 seeks to give ideas which can be put into practice immediately and will be particularly useful when dealing with students before you have had a chance to build up those vital long-term relationships. Section 6 deals with longer term strategies and Section 7 provides ideas for dealing with those types of problems which commonly occur in your teaching life.

In the role play section (Section 8), common problems can be performed by teachers in training sessions. The objective is to explore some commonly experienced and difficult behaviour problems and to bring them alive through role play. Teachers can then work out the best ways to deal with them through experimentation, discussion and reflection. The role plays include a mini script to set the scene and get the action going. Sometimes there are two versions which show contrasting approaches used by teachers. A series of probing questions for discussion are then posed.

Section 9 looks at the extreme behaviours and suggests techniques which I have found work well. The last section (Section 10) includes ideas which appear a little eccentric but are ones which over the years have produced great outcomes for me.

I am privileged to have received so much positive feedback from my previous books and training sessions and that has inspired me to write this new book. I hope you like it and find it useful.

Someone asked me recently, how I would sum up my own philosophy of dealing with behaviour management. That is a difficult question to answer in short. But here's my attempt: If you approach behaviour management with the 'I'm the teacher, do as I say or else' approach, then not only does it not work, but I doubt that it ever did. On the other hand, if you rely on being friendly and likeable, and harbour a hope that that will, of itself, be enough then, unfortunately you are, in my opinion, also destined for failure. My philosophy is a common sense middle ground. I try to be fair, understanding, caring and professional. I try to be calm and encouraging, cheerful and hopeful. But above all, I rely on learning thoroughly the craft, in all its meticulous and fascinating details. In this book I share with you the important aspects of that craft.

The fact that you are reading this book tells me something important about you as a teacher. You obviously have a desire to learn more and I know that if you continue with that desire and you are prepared to experiment and try new things, you may have down times, because all teachers do, but in the long run you will be successful. This is because the great news is that nobody is a born teacher. You can learn the craft if you work at it. I did and you can too! I wish you well in your career and I do hope you find, like I did, that the more you enhance your craft the more you will enjoy your job! And there's something even better. You'll find that your students, however badly behaved, will genuinely appreciate what you do.

Core Skills You Absolutely Must Learn

If a student makes a personal comment like: 'You like your food, don't you sir?' – how should you best deal with it?

If you are too soft in your reaction it is not long before other students join in. Unless you have a first-class relationship with the class, I would not recommend the laugh–it–off approach. A lot of students will see that as weakness.

Many teachers will react in a very strong way. This will rarely produce the best outcome. Very often an overreaction will invite the 'ring leaders' to say such things as: 'I was only joking about your weight!' Another student might then say: 'My dad's fatter than you anyway.' Now, because a conversation about your weight has arisen, this can soon escalate into a very nasty outcome.

Here is how a teacher might react for a better outcome: 'OK Barrie, I've heard what you're saying,' using a calm, firm voice. 'I'm pleased with how you get on in my lessons, most of the time.' Serious look held, eye to eye, for a few brief moments. Then say, 'But those personal comments cross the line. I won't have them.' Keep it brief, keep the serious look for a brief moment and now change back to the normal classroom persona of warm and enthusiastic with firm control. You say: 'OK, that's finished with that, good, now back to work.'

The tone must be businesslike. You then say something specific about the work, and then say: 'I want to have a look at Charlotte's and then I will work my way round and see a few more. Right, we have 6 minutes before the next task! Come on, let's see some good work!' Then get on with the business of the lesson.

You will find that the skilful use of language and correctly pitched attitude will minimize the likelihood of the problem recurring.

This technique has magic in it and works incredibly well. Very often with challenging students, it is hard to get them to listen at the beginning of the lesson to your instructions. Type out what you are going to say and keep it brief, but not too short. Hand a copy to each student. Explain that you are going to read the instructions and that you are going to pause and ask a student at random what the next word is.

You start reading and then pause and ask somebody, who you definitely know to be following, what the next word is. Then say: 'Excellent, you are following; now let's check that everyone is following.' Read on. Choose another person who you know will be following and say 'well done' and read on. You will find that this is many times more effective in holding the attention of a challenging class than just talking to them.

The following will enhance this idea:

1. Make sure that it is only one word that the student says in response to your question: 'What is the next word please Harry?' If they try to read on say: 'I want to read the links for this particular piece please and you'll get a chance to read later in the lesson.' This way you remain in control of the important pace of the activity.

2. If you can make the instructions an entertaining short story, it works even better. Any topic for any subject can be introduced by way of a short entertaining story if you use a bit of creative imagination.

3. Adding an interesting picture to the written word works even better. Note: I have found that a serious picture works better than a funny one. You can comment about a detail in the picture to hold attention.

Very often a class will work in a way that is far too noisy. Teachers will naturally try to solve this by reprimanding individual students, shouting, banging on the desk and continually nagging the whole class. The situation improves a little at first, but then the power of the class soon reverts to how it was. The teacher feels that he is against the whole class at this point.

So what do you do? I have found that 'the extended strategic scan' can work wonders. You stand in a strategic position in the classroom. You watch. If individual students ask for help at this stage, you say: 'I can't help you yet until the class is settled!' This is a crucial point.

You then start making strategic comments. You look to see where the distractions are coming from. Even in a very challenging class, it is usually only a few who you need to target. You then make specific short comments like: 'Stephen, put that away now!' Then you pause and look for a positive thing. You then say: 'Well done Stacey, you are working quietly, good.' You then target someone with another firm and short reprimand and so on. Give lots of pauses between comments.

Refuse to help anyone until the noise level is where you want it. Tell them that. Keep repeating: 'Noise too high, lower please. Lower please. Thank you.' You stand, you wait, you watch, you comment and you continually ask them to carry on quietly with the work.

Importantly you then start to say: 'That's much better. That's a lot quieter. Thank you.' Maintain substantial pauses between comments to let the whole class know that you are doing nothing except watching them. Each student becomes aware that they are under your watchful gaze and that you are going to maintain it until things have settled to the way you want them to be. Gradually you will find the class settles down.

THERE'S TENSION IN THE AIR

Teachers have a lot to think about when they enter a classroom. It is no wonder that so many teachers are so tense.

Of the many teachers I have observed, I have noticed that excessive tension is one of the biggest barriers to effective teaching and it exacerbates poor behaviour. Teachers with excessive tension talk too quickly. They overreact to minor misbehaviour. They forget to pause between instructions to allow things to sink in. When called over to help an individual student the whole experience is dealt with at a hurried pace. The teacher's tension brings about a collective tension in the students. Energy levels are burnt up.

Schools themselves are increasingly places full of tension. The message we are implicitly giving to our students is for them too, to become more tense.

It doesn't have to be this way.

A good idea is to have a pocket reminder checklist before each and every lesson. It is a great idea to refer to the list before the lesson. It is a habit that makes a teacher a tense teacher and it can be changed to a habit of becoming a relaxed, aware teacher. You will feel better in every way. Your students will react differently. The quality of learning will be greatly enhanced. The whole thing will feel so much more pleasant. You will feel less exhausted at the end of the lesson. Remember to read through the checklist and act on the advice each and every lesson.

The pocket reminder checklist is:

1. Just before the lesson, clear your mind for a few moments and slow yourself down.
2. Slow your breathing and clench and relax your hands a few times.
3. Picture in your mind a peaceful calm lesson.
4. Think of a student asking you a question. Allow yourself thinking time. Answer in a slower, interested way.
5. Allow spaces between things. Pause between things you say.
6. Develop a relaxed look and a smile.

Some teachers have a warm friendly approach. But if this is all the teacher has, there lurk certain dangers.

Say a teacher is doing fine, and the lesson is going well. A student suddenly says: 'Don't look at me like that! Your smile is creepy!' The teacher replies with his soft warm reply. He tries to smile the problem away. Then a friend joins in and goads others into joining in by saying: 'Yer, he looks at me a bit creepy. I think he's a weirdo . . . don't you?' The teacher stays calm and replies in a warm way. The students start to mock his voice and the teacher attempts to continue the lesson. The teacher now relies on the hope that things will quickly settle but the 'lead players' are watching him.

It is a core skill for a teacher that he must be able to switch his approach and challenge inappropriate behaviour, deliver an effective reprimand and then follow it up in a firm and determined way.

In our example the teacher may have moved a little towards the student and perhaps said : 'I hear what you're saying. Your behaviour is inappropriate and I would like it to stop immediately. We need to get back to our work.' You would deploy the firm, no nonsense, low voice, the confident body language and the attitude which says 'I have dealt with this many times and it does not bother me'.

Then, and only then, would he continue with his lesson, switching back to his predominantly warm mood. If the trouble continued he would, of course, have to go up the ladder of consequences as usual. The main point is that, in a situation as described, the teacher must challenge the inappropriate behaviour to stop it in its tracks. It is the carrying on in a warm friendly way, not challenging it, which will lead to an escalation and a highly unsatisfactory outcome.

THE DISCERNING EYE AND THE DISCERNING MIND

Develop a keen, discerning eye. The more years I teach the more I realize that it is the development of a discerning eye and a discerning mind which really counts.

The discerning eye is able to skim the class continually and, like a radar, be able to home in and distinguish potentially dangerous areas.

A discerning mind is knowing how to tackle a particular situation. Say, for example, the teacher becomes aware that a particular student is accused of stealing a memory card from another student's phone. There may well be witnesses on both sides of the argument and the potential for a row to erupt is enormous. However, you would be unwise to attempt to deal with this type of problem within a classroom setting. The whole thing will need to be properly and thoroughly investigated.

Your urgent function at that time is two things: (1) to ascertain just the names of who is involved and (2) to explain firmly and clearly that the lesson must continue and the situation will be thoroughly investigated by senior staff, directly the lesson finishes. Make quite a thing of writing down the names in your pocket notebook.

If the students involved persist in escalating the argument you must arrange for all of them to be removed from the room at once.

After the lesson, and as soon as convenient, send a full report to the appropriate staff requesting that the matter be thoroughly investigated.

Incidentally, I have known, on many occasions in situations like this for the students to rapidly resolve the situation quietly, between themselves, and earnestly request you not to involve further staff.

If you use your discerning eye to detect a problem such as this early on, and your discerning mind to decide the best way to deal with it, you will allow yourself space to continue with the your main task, which is to teach.

In the management of behaviour, never leave anything to chance. Have a system and method for all the core activities. For example, make sure you know how you want the students to enter the room. Make sure you know how you want them to leave. How materials will be given out and collected ? How will the time be used? Make sure that you allow plenty of time to collect everything up and make sure you have thought out how the various materials will be collected and where will they be stored.

If there is homework, you must have an effective system for giving it out and collecting it in. You must also know how to check if it doesn't come in and what to do with those who have not done their homework.

When you mark books, make sure you know how much will be done in the classroom and how much outside the classroom. With commendations, think through carefully exactly how you will manage them.

There are so many other things, of course, but the main point is that if you have simple and effective systems to deal with the predictable flow of work and activity, then, like all good managers, you will have freed yourself up to be able to deal with difficult unpredictable issues as and when they arise.

A great deal of poor behaviour management can be traced back to the simple fact that the teacher is working without effective systems and methods. In that way he is not managing the classroom at all but is reacting and he will have virtually no time or energy left to be able to tackle the challenging stuff, like behaviour.

SYSTEM, METHOD AND ORDER

It is of course a core skill to learn how to reprimand but teachers are of course very short on time and dealing with the paperwork involved in reprimands and formal reprimands can be very off-putting. Therefore, adapt a system where you can speak for a short time, after a lesson, with a particular student. It may be that you need to arrange in advance for another member of staff to be there to discourage the student from rushing off.

Students with challenging behaviours have a whole list of reasons why they can't even spare a minute and they are expert at being very convincing in this regard.

But you make them an offer. You explain that one minute now will save a lot of their time if the senior staff are involved.

You can then go through the reasons why you are unhappy and explain what you want to see in the next lesson. It is important to make a quick note of what is said in front of the student. You then, make it clear that if the behaviour improves next lesson then this note can be destroyed. If not, then you will have no choice but to write a formal report to the senior staff.

You must be certain to follow up in the next lesson. Congratulate, if improvements are seen, and likewise, fill out a full report if there is no improvement.

Also, if the student dashes off when you ask him to wait you must make sure that a senior member of staff contacts him about it that day, without fail or your system will not work at all.

In most cases this idea works very well, is quick to implement and saves a great deal of unnecessary paperwork and fuss. You are trying to nip a situation in the bud to prevent escalation.

Your greatest asset, as a teacher, is your voice. You must do everything you can to protect it. It is well known that teachers should hardly ever shout. But a lot of teachers quite simply talk too much. They give a running commentary throughout the lesson which acts like a kind of backdrop of sound. A lot of teachers feel that teaching is talking and so they talk all the time. Talking should be only a part of the teaching process.

For great behaviour management the less you say, and the more work your students do because of the way you have set things up, the better. It took me many years to realize that.

If you talk too much, what you say loses its effect. It also tires you out unnecessarily and puts a strain on your vocal chords.

The longer I have taught the more I have realized that you should organize things so that the necessity to talk is minimized. I have observed some teachers who stand at the front and talk for almost the whole lesson. If you look at the students, they are often in a very passive and docile state. They are almost resting. They are not learning much because they are not 'doing'.

If you observe a teacher who is great at behaviour management you will see the students actively working and the teacher circulating, watching, commenting, guiding, pointing out and above all, listening. She will be actively listening to what the students tell her and can therefore gauge how well they are understanding the materials. Her actual talking will be surprisingly minimal.

Obviously talking is a vital part of the teacher's toolkit. Become an expert on strategically using your voice for maximum effect. When you plan your lessons, think carefully about the stages of the lesson and how best to use your voice. It is, after all, your greatest asset.

BASIC TRAINING

An old Japanese Judo master was once asked how he had become so expert at Judo. His reply was: 'Three things: number 1 – basic training; number 2 – basic training and number 3 – basic training.' The point is that sometimes with behaviour management techniques we get so sophisticated that we forget the importance of basic training.

Every single time a class comes into your classroom use the same routine to get them seated and started. Every single time someone calls out, remind them of the rule. Every single time a student gets angry with you, respond in a calm controlled way. Every single time you give an instruction, use a warm friendly voice and an encouraging tone. However low and fed up you may feel, always act as if you're cheerful and positive. Forever be interested in the work you are teaching. Always deal with dangerous behaviour in a swift and determined way. Never allow swearing in your presence.

The above are of course a few main examples of basic training which together form the backbone of behaviour management.

But one item of basic training needs a special mention as a core skill which you absolutely must learn and always use to the maximum. It is quite simply the art of repetition.

Many of the behaviour problems I have observed can be directly traced back to a lack of repetition on the teacher's part. Often teachers assume too much.

If for example, you want the noise level lowered, don't just mention it once, tell them that you're going to ask in a moment for the noise to be lowered; ask them to lower the noise and then thank them for lowering the noise.

You vary the pattern of your language to avoid rigid boring repetition but the underlying principle remains. Repetition is absolutely key to behaviour management. Never forget to use the basic training.

Be One Step Ahead

Teachers often feel under pressure to provide a solution to all problems there and then. However, although the vast majority of situations can be effectively managed there and then, there is a hard core of certain problems which cannot be dealt with in this way. This is where a notebook and a particular way in which it can be used, is of immense help.

Take the following example:

A particular student is being deliberately and repeatedly antagonistic .You have carried out the normal types of reprimand but her behaviour remains the same and her attitude has hardened to a 'couldn't care less' one. This has been happening over several lessons and is, in fact getting worse. There is the temptation, on the part of the teacher, to react very sternly in an attempt to solve this problem once and for all. But it might be better to say this:

'Alice, I have asked you several times to stop antagonizing other students and you have completely ignored me. I'm not going to get into an argument with you. This is what I'm going to do . . . ' now, take out your notebook and open it up. Then say: 'I'm going to arrange a meeting with your head of year so that we can discuss this and get to the bottom of it. We can't carry on like this.' Then make a brief note and say: 'Now, I must get on with the lesson, there are plenty of students to see.' Then move away to another part of the room and get quickly involved in helping someone.

The fact that this is now written down has quite an impact on most students and that in itself is often enough to help modify the behaviour. The technique has the benefit of avoiding an argument and yet showing the whole class that bad behaviour will be dealt with.

Do, of course remember to follow it up!

INTERRUPTIONS TO LESSONS

Imagine that you have started a lesson. Suddenly the door opens and another teacher enters, clearly angry. She asks if she may have 'a word' with Michael. You agree and the teacher, in front of the whole class, commences a fearful, powerful and loud reprimand of Michael because of something dreadful he did at break. The teacher thanks you and leaves, feeling better that she has got it off her chest!

Michael now starts cursing the teacher and others join in. The important hard won peace is destroyed.

The solution to this problem, which is not uncommon, is to have agreements throughout the school about when it is the right time to disturb a lesson. In fact, when you analyse it, I would consider it to be a very substantial behaviour management issue when you take into account the effect of all interruptions on your lesson. Very often there are requests to allow students to leave your lesson for a number of reasons. There is considerable disruption when the student leaves and there is even worse disruption when the student returns.

In the vast majority of cases, the students could easily be spoken to after school or at some time other than lesson time. It is very tempting and convenient for students to be visited and dealt with for a huge range of reasons: everything from a missing piece of uniform to a fight at break time. My point is this. If your school is really serious about excellent behaviour management then agreements must be made to only disturb a lesson in a case of emergency. The system and organization of the school should be doing everything in its power to help you run smooth, uninterrupted lessons.

If it is a problem in your school, be one step ahead and try to arrange appointments with senior staff and discuss how the situation could be improved. Don't just live with it. The price you have to pay is very high.

When two classes or more work together for an event it can often lead to the worst behaviour management problems I have ever experienced and indeed the most frequent cause for serious complaints from parents.

The events might be to do with sports, or the rehearsal of a play or concert, or an event connected to an outside visitor and so on.

Teachers are busy people and often the plans for the event are made in a hasty way. It is also believed by many that there are just too many 'what ifs' to possibly cover every contingency. Therefore plans are often loose.

But when a large group of students are assembled in an unfamiliar situation it is absolutely vital that thorough and detailed preparation is completed. If not, it would be safer not to have the event at all.

Most of the things that go wrong stem from confusion and uncertainty. Ninety per cent or more of the problems which cause trouble are completely predictable and the fact that there are no arrangements in place to deal with the problems, as they arise, leads to a situation which is completely avoidable.

The teachers responsible for organizing the event must be given the time to sit down and plan through the stages, in detail, asking questions like: 'Where do the students go after activity one has finished ?' 'What if they have no uniform?' 'What do we do if a student refuses to take part?' The details of predictable common problems must be thought through and then a session must be held with all the staff involved so that the details of the plans can be fully explained.

All this sounds very obvious, but it is incredible to me how often in practice teachers, because of the pressures of lack of time, do not carry out the planning and communicate it clearly to all concerned. It is amazing how often a simple thing could have saved a great deal of trouble, if only it had been thought through in advance.

THE IMPORTANCE OF FEEDBACK

I would like you to take a moment to think about the best teacher you ever had. Can you picture that person clearly in your mind? Now, this is the question. Did you ever tell that teacher what you thought? I'm willing to guess that in most cases the answer will be no.

In the world of work we rely on feedback. It gives us reassurance about how we're doing. When I worked in a bank I was given feedback continually from a whole range of sources. It gave me confidence.

In teaching, I have always been surprised at how little feedback we get. Yes, there are inspections and various observations, but compared to the bulk of what we do, the feedback is tiny. You may, by chance, hear a comment from a student that they like your lessons, but there is a sense of randomness about it.

I have developed a way of getting useful feedback from the students. You carefully design a 'customer service' style questionnaire and get your students to fill it in. You may well not use it for all classes and you perhaps wouldn't want to use it too frequently. However, when used strategically it can give you vital information which would be otherwise completely unknown.

The types of questions might be like the following:

1. What do you enjoy doing best in this lesson?
2. What types of task would you like to do more of?
3. What types of tasks do you do in other lessons which you enjoy?

When you introduce new ideas into your teaching you can tell your students that it is based on ideas that they have given you. It shows that you care. More than that, it shows that you are forever striving to always be 'one step ahead' by keeping in tune with what your students like.

A teacher has an overload of information coming at him from a wide range of sources. Some of the biggest problems and disruptions in behaviour management can arise when a busy teacher simply doesn't know exactly what is going on. Half the class doesn't turn up and you find out from other students that there is a play rehearsal. Ten minutes into a lesson, ten students are called out to have an inoculation. Your lesson is going well when the whole class is called for a photograph session. In a school year the variety of reasons for changes to plan is quite amazing.

Yes, there are of course memos and emails and meetings galore, but in practice I have developed a simple little system which is worth its weight in gold.

You build up a small network of key people. For example, your deputy head of department, your year head and maybe the receptionist. You work out lines of communication so that all major activities which occur in the annual calendar are covered and these key people are aware of them.

Then you develop the habit each and every day of just double-checking exactly what is going on the next day with each of the key people. It only takes a few moments but you will be amazed at how many things you will pick up which may well have otherwise slipped through the communication net. It will give you an early warning and therefore vital preparation time.

It is important to check the day before, because so many plans printed in advance in notices are often changed at the last minute. This system picks that up.

As a technique for behaviour management it will help with your structural organization and thereby give you more time, confidence and control over the details of the day.

A WAY TO BE SURE YOU KNOW WHAT IS GOING ON

HOW TO MAGNIFY YOUR VIGILANCE

If students know, in advance, that you have a regular system for checking up on the work that they do, then they will work much better. As a general principle, the more someone knows that they will be monitored, within reason, the more it helps automatically with behaviour management.

In practice a lot of teachers are quite random in the way they check up on their students' work. They may look at certain students' work and not others. The reason for this is that it is very time consuming to monitor everyone's work in every lesson. Also, in a busy classroom all sorts of forces are at work. Certain students command your attention and help more than others.

The solution is to have a system which can work alongside other ways of checking their work. Have a short session, perhaps halfway through the lesson where you can announce in a cheerful enthusiastic voice: 'It's time for self assessment of progress time!'

You would have trained your students, in previous lessons, on how to reflect on their own work and give themselves a mark out of ten for how well they think they're doing. You teach them how to quickly assess their work to gain an overall impression. You show them clearly what a three out of ten might look like compared to say, a nine out of ten.

Make the session fun and quick fire. Have a copy of the seating plan and call round the class jotting down the marks rapidly against the names.

The great thing about this is that is builds up trust, the students enjoy it and it saves time and alerts the teacher to move in on a problem area straight away. It helps focus the students to actively think about their progress in an effective, snappy and regular way. You'll be surprised how accurate they are and the beauty is that it magnifies the teacher's vigilance.

One of the greatest ways of controlling behaviour is to be one step ahead and stop the behaviour from becoming a problem in the first place. To do this, I find that you must develop an 'omniscient presence' in the classroom.

This is where the students are always aware of your overseeing, guiding presence. It is your presence which has a strong deterrent effect on bad behaviour and at the same time exudes an encouraging feel for good work. You do not achieve this through shouting, talking continuously or blustering around. You use quiet controlled strategy.

For example, be sure to move around the class and make quiet comments to students. Frequently let them know that you know what is going on. Give feedback, quietly, on the various things you've noticed. Stand at the back and just watch. Make the odd comment. Make use of the space in the room to move around into all areas of the classroom. Comment from various parts of the room so the students get used to you being everywhere.

By a careful combination of little things you will create a huge sense of presence and awareness. You will also be in a position to spot things early and move in and quietly settle things down. You will also be able to create a sense of momentum and pace. You let them know sometimes explicitly, more often implicitly, that you are with them every step of the way. You will be really managing what happens in your classroom.

When you build in your 'signposts' and explain how pleased you are and remind the whole class of where they should be and what is the next task, at certain key points in the lesson, then the cumulative effect of your presence becomes very powerful.

So explore ways to fill the room with your presence by strategically using as little effort on your part to produce in return maximum results on their part.

WHAT HAPPENS NEXT TIME?

It often surprises me that when a student goes through a reprimand procedure the structure almost always deals first with what went wrong and second with what the punishment consequences should be. Should the punishment be a detention? Should the writing be cleaned off the wall? There is often an absence of a third stage. The third stage is how can we both (student and teacher) turn this disadvantage into an advantage?

Instead of seeing the student as an 'offender', see him as 'in training'. It really is a great opportunity to get to know the student better in reference to what went wrong.

Supposing, for example, the student had lost his temper and punched the wall and kicked stuff about. Here's a great time to chat about what causes you to lose your temper. You can point out that it is a human condition. That sometimes you are wound up so much that you lose your temper. You, of course, can take the opportunity to explain the dangers of losing control and how dreadful the consequences could become. You then work out what to do if it happens again.

But the main point here is that now there is a shared understanding. If you notice that the student is losing his temper next time you can immediately intervene and refer to the useful things we learnt last time. Because you have already been through the problems with this student in a calm and considered way, it helps enormously when the problem recurs.

You can say things like: 'Do you remember Jack? Didn't we agree that you should go for a short walk and calm down?' The shared understanding, memory of the meeting and enhanced relationship will help with a successful outcome in a difficult, stressful situation.

So when you reprimand, reflect, punish and don't forget to work out with the student a plan as to how to cope the next time around.

Being one step ahead can be enhanced enormously by operating systems for management of behaviour which click in smoothly and effectively. Every teacher knows that having good routines avoids the extra energy required by the teacher to keep reminding students what to do at certain key times of the lesson.

Using symbols works amazingly well in supporting and maintaining those routines. Supposing your students are in the settling down stage but many of them are a bit slack and bags are on desks and several are chatting and so on. Show them a large symbol. Hold it up and ask someone to say what it means. Supposing you have a simple picture of a desk in colour with the number five above it. This could be on a large card which you hold up.

You ask one of them what the symbols means. They will say: 'Coats on the back of chairs; pens out on desk; bags neatly under desk; arms folded ready to begin!' The symbol triggers the response. The more you show it, the more you repeat it, the more efficiently the class responds. By getting someone to say what the symbol means, you can then repeat it with an attitude of praise: 'Well done, you remembered all five things!' And then say them again. Pause, as normal, between each one to check round the room to ensure that everyone is responding.

You can, for example, have symbols for these key points in the lesson. I suggest:

1. Settling down at start
2. Changing activities
3. Whole class listening to teacher
4. Noise level
5. Finishing off routine

They work well because they have the power of a company logo with instant recognition which powerfully triggers all the things that they know will inevitably follow. They re-enforce the routines which are in place. They save you a lot of time and energy. They make a big contribution to the smooth running of the lesson and help enormously with smooth behaviour management.

RESEARCH WHICH PAYS HUGE REWARDS

This idea does take some research and effort. I reserve it for students with very challenging behaviour.

Firstly, spend a lot of time talking to subject teachers about the small group of students whom you find particularly challenging. Find out how they behave in their lessons and build up a knowledge of how they're doing across the school. Particularly ask the teachers to be kind enough to give you brief regular updates of anything interesting in this area. Short emails are fine. A few specific up to date details of things they've done well in other subjects are vital.

When you have particularly difficult experiences with those students, have a quiet word with them on a brief and regular basis. Now here is the crucial thing, and is the reason why the idea works so well. Chat with them about their behaviour, not so much as it was in your lesson, but as it is across the school. Put the whole focus on the improvements, however slight.

You might say: 'Duncan, I see you're doing well in Science. Things are much better for you there. Not such a great lesson with me today, what with all that shouting out and everything. Anyway, let's not get bogged down in all that again. Let's look at the whole picture. Mr Smith is also delighted with the work you did in Technology. Well done Duncan, you must be pleased. I really am looking forward to being able to praise you up in my subject. I know we can do it!'

The student doesn't know how much you know about him but suspects that it is an awful lot. Something deep down in human nature is triggered if you use this idea carefully. The student feels a sort of obligation to improve in your lesson because you're being kind enough to praise him for work done well elsewhere.

It's Not What You Teach, It's How You Teach It

Here's an idea which has helped me enrich my own teaching and has also enhanced holding the attention of the class on many occasions. In my book *100+ Ideas for Managing Behaviour* I mentioned the importance of exchanging behaviour management ideas between subject areas. In addition to this, an exchange of actual methods of teaching between subject areas can also be of great benefit.

Make it a habit to regularly chat with teachers from other subject areas and ask them what parts of their lessons work particularly well with their students. Focus particularly on how that part of the subject was actually taught. You can then make notes about this and adapt and style some of your own subject content into the forms which have worked so well in other areas.

When you present the idea to the class you say something like: 'I've had a chat with the Geography Department and I understand that you enjoy building up a whole class map and it works well with you. So today, what I'm going to try to do, with your help, is to build up a class map to show the maths processes which we have covered.'

With a little bit of creative imagination it is truly amazing how subject content can be packaged and moulded into endless ideas for how it is actually presented and taught.

With this idea you build relationships between colleagues and once again demonstrate to the students that you are willing to find out about things they enjoy doing.

This idea is particularly good at managing behaviour because one of the great antidotes for poor behaviour is to hold the attention of the student with interesting and demanding material. When the students finds that they can use skills which they developed in other lessons it gives the work an enhanced status and makes it much more interesting.

A GREAT WAY TO PRODUCTIVELY HARNESS THEIR ENERGY

Very often poor behaviour can be the result of students' excessive nervous energy which needs working off.

A great way to do this is with an 'active quiz'. A good way to arrange this is to divide the class into two and call them team A and team B. You then ask for one volunteer from each group. You explain that they have to come up to the front and perform a task, as representative of their team and in competition with a volunteer from the opposing team.

It is important to make it clear that only students who sit quietly will be chosen, and that if you don't get chosen this time you may well get a chance in the next round. This is a powerful way to control behaviour.

It is also important to keep to a format. Invite two volunteers to the front. Hand them a board writer each. Have some nice music ready to play and say that they have exactly one minute to draw a mystery object and the teacher, as judge, will allocate a mark out of ten. You then 'cue' them to get ready and say: 'Right, you have one minute to see who can draw the best mobile phone. Ready, steady, go!'

When the minute is up take the pens back, ask them to return to their seats and make a big thing of allocating marks which you record onto a highly visible score chart. You then ask for more volunteers.

You can be very creative in the tasks they perform and of course can link it to the work you are doing. The important thing is to control the process carefully and you will find it uses their energy in a very positive way and is brilliant at evoking a mood of fun which helps manage their behaviour.

With a certain use of creative thought you can adapt any information into an active way of learning. All teachers know that when you talk or show or tell students information, they are in a very passive position and that is not always best for learning or indeed for managing poor behaviour. By introducing activity and fun you can truly bring things alive and make them memorable.

In practice, however, the problem is often that teachers introduce active tasks, find that it all degenerates into pandemonium and therefore understandably return to traditional safe teaching with tried and tested methods.

But I have found a halfway house which works well. You write, (or arrange with your colleagues from the English department) a short mini play which the students read and act out. Here's a very short example. Supposing you were teaching the idea in science that the further an object falls in a vacuum, the faster it goes. You need to explain that it is air pressure which works against this acceleration of speed.

MINI PLAY RAINDROPS

Two raindrops are falling from the clouds. The students act as raindrops. A = raindrop 1; B = raindrop 2.

A: I'm going faster and faster down to the ground. Look at the view.

B: Yes, but notice how we are slowing down a bit.

A: Why's that?

B: It's the air pressure slowing us down.

A: What's that ?

B: It's invisible and you can't see it but the air is all around us.

A: Why can't we see it ?

Do you get the idea? The students love scenarios which are surreal. Once you've started with a mini script they often improvise the rest, actively using what they know.

After the role play you can recap key learning points from what they did and indeed run it through again with different students acting in a different way. It's great fun and it bridges the gap between chaotic active learning and controlled useful active learning.

HOW TO BRING INFORMATION ALIVE

THE MAGIC OF MYSTERIES

One of the things I have found that never fails to capture interest is a good mystery, if it is intriguingly presented.

You can manage a lot of bad behaviour by using this technique. You choose a mystery and research it. It is especially great if you have a set of pictures to project up on the screen.

In time you can build up a portfolio of suitable mysteries. Some that I have used with great success are: 'The Loch Ness Monster'; 'UFOs'; 'Ghosts'; 'Stonehenge'. With a little bit of creative imagination you can provide a meaningful link with the main body of your lesson. It also wonderfully encourages the students to contribute their own ideas and gets them settled, ready for working on the next part of the lesson. You can also use it as a reward by saying that if the objectives of the lesson are met then they can return to the mystery at the end of the lesson.

You start your presentation by talking about a picture which you have up on the screen. The key thing is to show that you are intrigued. You suggest possible explanations and you refer to what other people have suggested. But you say that it remains a mystery. You then ask the class what they think and as they contribute you add in more and more intriguing information.

Say you had a picture of the 'Marie Celeste' on the screen, you could say things like: 'Where did all the crew go? The galley was all set up ready for breakfast. Eggs with the tops cut off, all ready. Where did they go?' By sounding mystified yourself you will draw them in.

One of the hardest parts of a lesson is engaging interest. With students with challenging behaviour, it is a good idea to hook them in immediately. One of the great things about this technique is that it firmly gets the attention of the class thereby making it easier to lead in to the next activity.

One of the most effective ways I have found is to tell a story that pulls them all in. The way to do this is to devise a story that starts with a problem. You can creatively link this to the main part of your lesson. Say, for example, you wanted to teach them about the weather of South America. You devise a story about a traveller who has a journey down the Amazon. If you can have a suitable picture projected up on the screen to set the mood then so much the better. A sound track with the sounds of the forest playing would enrich the experience even more.

Now, you have ready a set of small cards with numbers on one side and short phrases or words on the other. Each student is handed a card as they come in and you say: 'Don't lose that. You need to use that in a moment.' Each card is different. One, for example may say: 1 'humid'.

You have the master copy of the story with the key parts of it numbered and a note of what each card says.

Then you plunge into your story. You may say: 'Now Martin was rowing down the Amazon River but he had a big problem. His clothes were wet because it was so . . . then say- who has card 1? Please read it out. Yes, well done - 'humid', you know that's when the air's all hot and sticky . . . anyway he rows on and then he sees something amazing. Who has card number 2?' And so on.

It is a great way to involve everyone from the start.

Teachers know that the more you can take the attention from yourself and get the students to concentrate on the task, the better it is for both behaviour management and learning.

However, with a lot of 'student-centred tasks', or group work activities, you find in practice that many lazy students hide behind the work done by others.

Many teachers counteract this situation by creating a rather tense atmosphere. They walk round and make comments like: 'Come on Peter, you've hardly done anything, get on with it . . . ' and so on. That doesn't enhance the learning experience. The behaviour management may seem better because the focus is off the teacher, but there often isn't much good learning going on.

In this type of learning situation the teacher must become the 'hub' of a wheel. He must facilitate the learning by providing the materials and tasks, but it is of vital importance that he also sets up an 'atmosphere of enquiry'. He must use praise and continually share and broadcast good work to engender a sense of busy excitement .

He must encourage the act of asking questions and getting students to jot down their questions as they explore the task. He can make connections between parts of the classroom as the lesson progresses by saying things like: 'Listen everyone, this is brilliant. Tracy wrote down a question earlier 'what is a tangent' and I've just noticed that Andrew over here is working on an answer to that right now.'

You will find that the atmosphere of the whole group will encourage everyone to take part and the more you spot good work and broadcast it, the more the students will join in. Make sure you have check lists and a variety of information freely available and always be clear about the task you are all working towards.

Also make sure that you have key signposts during the process where you draw the attention of the whole class to the progress being made.

As I've often said, one of the key elements with behaviour management is getting students interested in the work. If you have not got enthusiasm for what you are teaching how can you expect the students to have any interest in the work you ask them to do? The longer I teach, the more I realise that it is the teacher's passion for the subject which rubs off on the students. They will want to know what it is about the subject that you find so fascinating.

Don't forget to include lots of phrases like, 'now, the really interesting thing about this is . . .' and 'I don't know about you, but I find this bit fascinating! Just think for a moment. How is it that . . . .'

You will be met with a lot of negative reactive comments like: 'How's that interesting? It's boring!' But the key thing is to carry on with your enthusiastic attitude and language. You strongly anticipate, in the way you speak to them, that they will soon become fascinated too. Do not be put off by their reaction whatsoever.

As a preparation before each lesson, remember to go through thinking about the interesting aspects and how to amplify them and make them sound even more interesting.

Think about other materials you could use to up the interest levels further.

Think back to why you got interested in the subject yourself and bring that passion to bear in how you talk and your whole attitude.

We are living at a time when there has never been so much information available and in a way that is part of the problem. Students have access to so much information that there is the danger that it can all be viewed in the same flat and dull way. It is a primary job for you as a teacher to select information from the ocean available and teach the students how to be selective, become fascinated and enjoy knowledge. If you don't, who will?

A very common problem that must be tackled in the short term is the way a large part of a challenging class does not listen carefully to your instructions. With many classes with poor behaviour, it is the lack of listening skills which is one of the critical things which contributes to how difficult it can be to teach them. A wonderful technique which you can use straight away is to introduce a bit of fun and also make the listening immediately active.

You explain nicely and clearly that you are going to give them a little bit of information in a few moments. You say: 'I wonder who, in this room, can show me how good their memory is. I'm going to ask you a couple of things (try to avoid the word "questions") and see if you can remember. Sometimes I'm amazed at how good your memories are at your age. Let's see how well you can do today.'

You then present the information and give a small pause which builds a little bit of atmosphere. You then ask a few questions (try to make the first ones really easy and then get to the harder ones) and you really congratulate the students who can put their hands up and give the answers. Be careful to say things like, 'nearly there, can anyone add a tiny bit to that? . . . '

You will find that the technique is immediately effective with a new class and gives the lesson an initial boost.

Also, by splitting the information into two chunks, after the first session it works well to say: 'That was great! I noticed a few people, however, didn't say that much. Let's have one more quick go at this and see if everyone can remember something this time!' You are therefore making the delivery of information more active and you will find that the second session works even better than the first because everyone now knows what to do.

All over the world and down through the ages the standard model for teaching has of course been the teacher standing at the front while the students sit and listen.

It took me a long time to realize and develop a way of getting the students to help me present information. Sometimes, if too many students get involved and they are not clear about exactly what to do then it can all become a bit chaotic, scares the teacher off and results in a reverting back to firm traditional models.

But with the use of a certain process and some care in how it is organized, getting students to help you present, can work wonders in helping with behaviour management.

I ask for volunteers and explain that I would like them to come up to the board, or sit at my computer to type information for projection onto the white board. I usually choose one or two students and explain that it is useful for them to write key words to emphasize points while I teach the class.

Key words and short phrases works better than lots of information. I explain something to the class and then ask the student to write the key word or phrase for me.

It helps with behaviour management because it automatically keeps the class quieter. You say: 'I'm going to choose the next person to help me but I will only choose a quiet one!'

It also helps because you are involving them, which makes the learning more fun and active. You can look at the key word and refer to it and use it as a focus point.

At the point of transition from teaching the whole class to the change of activity where the students work on their own tasks, you can say: 'When we sum up later, I might need some more volunteers to help me present some key points. It will help me to choose people if you work well.'

HOW STUDENTS CAN HELP YOUR PRESENTATION

THE BEST WAY OF TEACHING

There is an old Chinese Proverb which says: 'To teach is to learn twice'. It is well known that various types of teaching have various levels of effectiveness from passively listening to actively doing. But the most effective way to learn is to teach someone else what you know.

If you can set up in your classroom frequent opportunities for the students to teach each other, then it accelerates what they learn and by making the nature of the work interesting and dynamic, it automatically improves behaviour management. By giving students teaching opportunities it helps them to usefully channel their excess energy and it also helps with confidence building.

But there is a caution to note. A lot of teaching which I have observed where one student teaches another is often based on the brighter student helping out the student who needs a bit more help.

There are many ways of organizing it so that it gets away from that model. For example, organize tasks where students need certain information and knowledge from other students. Arrange your resource materials so that different students get different materials.

A brief example of this would be to consider a whole class task where the aim is to discover about life in Elizabethan London. Different students are allocated specialist areas of research, say food, housing, entertainment and all the students have to produce a key point information sheet which covers the whole thing. In order to get that key point information they have to learn it from other students.

Once the overall set up has been organized, it then becomes the teacher's job to manage and facilitate and encourage students to teach each other.

Often this works so well that you can cue the class to listen to a particular student who will then teach the whole class about a particular aspect of the project.

The Language and Attitude of Success

This is a very challenging problem. Some students seem to have no interest in the work you set them.

Firstly, go through your normal tried and tested techniques. If they show no interest after a series of lessons, keep them back for a brief chat.

Explain that you have noticed the lack of interest and ask them why. The usual response is that they find the work boring.

With careful questioning you can find out what subjects they are good at. There is always something that they are good at. It may take a few little chats over a few lessons but eventually they will tell you what it is that they are good at. Supposing you teach English and a particular student is good at Geography, hold a conversation along these lines:

'Peter, I've been thinking, how about if I designed some work for you, to do with the book we're reading, but getting you to draw out a map and so that you can show me your map making skills?'

Next lesson, give out the work including Peter's map idea. Make a point of seeing if there is any improvement in his work and acknowledge it and show how pleased you are. It may take a few attempts to see improvements.

You can then use the improved work as a basis for discussing how else they might use other skills to help them. Keep following up, to show you have noticed and care, lesson after lesson.

It may seem a lot of trouble to go to and you may wonder how on earth you could find the time to individually design work when you have so many students to deal with. However, this idea is for the very rare case of the student who shows no interest even after you have tried all your usual techniques.

THE STUDENT WHO REALLY HAS NO INTEREST AT ALL IN DOING THE WORK

THE HOLISTIC PRAISE

If you have a student, who despite his best efforts, scores very low, this can have a very demotivating effect on the student. This is particularly true where a culture has arisen where exam results seem like the be all and end all of everything. It can have an isolating effect on the low achiever.

I have found that you need to carefully put the whole thing into perspective, and skilfully reframe the situation for the student. We have to be careful here with our use of language and present a 'holistic' picture. You gather together all the things which you know the student is good at and then you bring in some recent improvements and emphasize the effort and persistence aspect.

So you may say something, perhaps at a parents evening, like this: 'OK, of course we live in a world where exam results are a key factor. But Simon has definitely tried his best and the results he has got are the best we can manage at this time. But Simon has got a lot going for him. For example, he is very creative in his ideas. For example, the other day I set the class the following problem and Simon suggested the following, which was very good. Now that may not show up straight away in an exam result but, believe me, it is a vital life skill!'

Another important element of this approach is to have a running conversation with the student, over a series of lessons, about life skills. A great motivator is to find examples, and there are many, of people who struggled at school and then went on to achieve all sorts of great things. You can look at the biographies of such people and point put how they engaged with problem solving in their own way.

By taking such a holistic approach you will build a good relationship with your students and help give them confidence and encouragement.

As you become a more experienced teacher you realize more and more that it is the way you use language which is crucial in controlling behaviour. This is well known. However, there is a sort of sub-group of language skills in a classroom which I would identify as 'tennis banter' which is of great importance. It is to do with the way a teacher can re-frame students' comments to turn negative perceptions into positive ones. It is like tennis because the student serves you a ball and you return the serve to them. So for example, a common comment is: 'This work is boring' and a suitable reframing comment would be: 'How can we make this more interesting?' Or, 'in what ways would you like to work on this to bring it alive a bit? Perhaps you could . . .' and so on.

The great thing about this technique is that it keeps the momentum of the lesson going; it provides more energy in the mood of the lesson; it does not resist and reprimand negative comments but uses the flow and energy from this technique in a more productive way; it helps create a positive habit of response in the teacher which is a great asset and lastly, over time, it works away at the negative attitudes of some students to usher and nudge them gently into more positive frames of mind.

As a more advanced use of this, you can praise the students for their comments in a careful way, as if praising them for a good serve in tennis and then return the ball in such a way as to get them thinking.

For example, if a student said: 'There's too much here to read', reply with: 'A good observation Harry! Well done. I think you're right. How could we break this up into chunks to make it more manageable and clearer for us to work on? Maybe we could . . .' and so on.

With a really challenging student, where all traditional techniques seem to fail or be ineffective I have developed, over the years, a technique which, although not perfect, does help to bridge the gulf between what you get and what you want.

This is how it works. You take the student to one side at the end of the lesson. This in itself can be tricky, as challenging students are often anxious about time and want to rush off. You make it clear in a firm but friendly way that the present situation is totally not working. You explain that together, you and the student, have a problem to solve and you ask the student for suggestions about how things could be better. If you are brave enough to try this I think you will find that nine times out of ten the student will suggest something which you can try to take on board in order to manage the situation better.

The power of this technique is that the student will see you trying to compromise. You need to be persistent, calm and you need to draw attention in future lessons to what it is you're trying to do. You can review progress and say how pleased you are, even if only a tiny improvement is made. The technique gives the student some say in the situation and helps to build respect between the two of you.

The ideas and suggestions you work with can be small things. For example the student may say: 'You stand over me and I want you out of my face!' So when next controlling behaviour, you can point out that you are talking 'from a distance, as agreed!' This allows an invisible energy and 'agreement' to start to bond between you.

This technique is reserved for behaviours which don't seem to respond to much else, and if used sparingly, carefully and sensibly it can be very powerful.

Imagine this situation. A teacher approaches a student who is obviously unhappy.

T = Teacher   S = Student

T: Are you OK, you seem to be scribbling frantically on your book?

S: I hate this school, it's rubbish.

T: Come on now, don't be like that, this is a really good school you know.

S: What's good about it ?

T: Well, lots of things. What about our new refectory, that's good isn't it ?

S: The food makes me sick I hate it. The dinner ladies keep picking on me. They're rubbish!

T: OK then, what about . . . .

You get the idea. Every time the teacher offers up reasons to be cheerful the student uses them as a platform to make even more negative comments about the school. It is effectively allowing a conversation to take place where the student feels that he has a free rein to speak out and criticize the school and all its teachers as he wants, adding insulting language to fuel his own dissatisfaction.

So how do you handle a conversation like this ? I have found that the best way to deal with this type of conversation is to strategically take control. Instead of offering lots of things you hope will change his mind, start reframing everything by asking questions like: 'What would you like to see here?' and 'How would you make changes then?' Listen to what he says and then start agreeing and commenting with things like: 'That's a good idea', or 'That's interesting , perhaps I could speak to the head about your thoughts?'

You will find that this transforms the temperature of the conversation. It will no longer be based on conflict and instead you will have areas of agreement and his mood will change and become more positive.

To be able to carefully manage conversations like this is a really useful part of a teacher's skill as it can help to lay positive foundation stones for the next conversation.

MAKING ABSTRACT RULES SEEM CONCRETE

I find if you give specific illustrations of things that can go wrong, it will powerfully support your rules. If you say: 'Don't throw pencils!', it can have much more impact if you say that you knew of a boy who lost his eye because a pencil was thrown across the room at him. It then makes an abstract rule become concrete.

You don't have to make all your illustrations so dramatic. If a student has a bag on their desk and the rule is to keep it on the floor under the desk, then explain, in a friendly way, the reason why. You might say: 'I've glimpsed some lovely looking sweets in your bag and if you stick it under your desk you won't be tempted to break the eating rule, will you?' You are much more likely to persuade them to comply by giving a sensible reason.

If a student is talking and others interrupt, it is very effective to say: 'I love discussions with this class, I really do. But if we don't keep to the rule of one at a time then I can't hear your wonderful ideas, can I?'

The habit of reminding students about why we have particular rules seems to help remove the confrontational nature of the communication and instead introduces a cooperative and caring atmosphere. Rather than the rules being seen as a barrier, they become seen as a sensible idea.

It is not necessary to always illustrate rules with specific examples but to do so now and then certainly helps what you say.

When you teach poorly behaved students who have low ability you can often sense a disabling mood of failure in all they do. Often the education system itself, which overtly singles out and recognizes high academic achievement above all else, can add to this mood of failure.

The way to turn this round is to constantly re-define exactly what success is, as far as you're concerned, and explain that you will be actively looking out for it all the time. You link the idea of success to effort, improvements and to a whole host of things important in life itself. You then look out for them and give positive feedback regularly and with enthusiasm.

You may say: 'That's great the way you had kind thoughts about that news item Naomi.' You might notice that Elliot's uniform is smarter than last lesson. Tell him! Be pleased. Keep looking, keep praising. Tell your class regularly that: 'All these little good things will eventually add up to huge things. I promise you they will!'

Look out for examples of life skills. If someone is polite, praise them. If someone asks an interesting question, be pleased and explain that the asking of good questions is vital to good learning. If someone sticks at a problem for quite a while, even if they don't solve it, praise them for keeping with it!

You build up a strong belief that it is not just results you are looking for to define success but the processes. You show them that we are all at various points on the learning road and it is keeping going that matters.

If you are constant and persistent with this idea you will notice that the mood of failure will surely evaporate like the morning mist and you will unleash an amazing power. The class will regain confidence and then anything is possible.

DESCRIPTION COMPARISON

Many teachers, when keeping a student after the lesson for a reprimand, will ask the student to write down what happened and why. This is an excellent technique to use. It allows the student to express their own feelings and the writing becomes a good focus for discussion. It is a more productive use of time than say, copying a dictionary.

But the problem is that almost always, that will be the end of it. The student's note will then be discarded.

I have found a way to get maximum advantage from this time. You keep the note and a few lessons later you call the student back for a short chat, read back the note to them and then point out specifically how things have improved. It works even better if you take the time and trouble to write a short updated description of the student's behaviour and when the two are read alongside each other it gives powerful proof of progress.

Another good system to develop, as an extension of this idea, is to regularly keep students back, for a short time, to confirm improvements in their behaviour. Make the emphasis praise. It sets up a nice atmosphere because the students know that when you ask them to stay back, the chances are that it is to praise rather than reprimand.

Your reputation as a fair and positive teacher who always looks for good things will be enhanced by using this idea.

When I meet students who are now adults and who used to be in my challenging classes, the most frequent reference they make to things they remember from my lessons years ago are the 'Mini talks on Motivational People!'

I have built up a considerable collection of biographies of people I admire who have achieved great success against horrendous odds. My examples include a man who was nearly burnt to death in an accident and now motivates people all round the world with his story; a rugby player who despite being paralysed still coaches rugby; a man who left school with no qualifications and set up a multimillion pound business; a person who was in prison as a young offender who went on to found a international magazine to help the homeless and many more.

I find that students who display difficult behaviour often feel that they are no good at anything and their own self-worth is low. When I present these mini talks I try to make them interesting by showing pictures and presenting the whole thing as an interesting story. I engage the students in the details of the problems the person experienced and then show them how he eventually triumphed over them.

If presented in a certain way the stories, because they are true, connect deep down with the common humanity and the power of the human spirit. I teach them that a positive mental attitude is what really matters in achieving things. By example, I show them what others have done and what is possible.

Often the stories help put their own problems into a kind of perspective and they act as deep motivators to work harder and try more. The stories themselves hold the interest of the students in quite an amazing way. They usually ask lots of questions.

I recommend that all teachers keep a supply of motivational mini talks to fire up students when things get low. They may not seem to work immediately but you are sowing a seed which will last forever.

Before you start a lesson, make sure you have looked through the work your students did the lesson before and make a list of names of those who did well and briefly, specifically why they did well. Also make a note of those who could have done much better.

When the lesson begins, put in an enthusiastic upbeat voice, why you are so happy. You could say: 'Do you know why I'm so happy? I've just been looking through the work you did last lesson. And guess what? It's really great!'

Then rapidly mention a few names and reasons. For example: 'Emma, you finished all the tasks, so did quite a few others. Brooklyn, your presentation was brilliant! Sean, I noticed that you decided to tackle the difficult questions. Well done!'

Then, almost casually, mention a couple of people who perhaps could try harder: 'Isaac, you perhaps didn't have a lesson as good as you normally do. But if I know you, you'll be doing more today. Am I right?'

Then finish off with a particular mention of more great work. For example: 'I can't go through all the good work, there's so much of it but I must lastly mention you Tyler. What a great illustration. Fantastic.'

Then quickly give out the work and get started on the lesson. By using this technique you start the lesson in a strong and positive way. There is a built in expectation of good work to be done today.

If you haven't had time to mark the books in detail, this gives a rapid and useful overview and shows your students that you are interested in their work. Also, the students who haven't done so well have not been embarrassed in any way but nevertheless have got the message that you expect even better things today.

For Immediate Effect

The first few lessons with a new group must be managed particularly carefully as they lay important foundations. I have known teachers to pitch in straight away with a really friendly approach, perhaps even cracking jokes and attempting to win the students over with the strength of their personality. Be cautious here. Sometimes a core of challenging students will use this very much to their advantage in trying to take early control of the lesson.

On the other hand I have also seen teachers go in like a regimental sergeant major and then wonder why little Emily is crying, only to find out that she is frightened!

It is well worth preparing in your mind how you are going to act in those vital first few lessons. You must be confident. You must use body language which shows solid authority. Your voice must be calm, assertive and encouraging. The students are watching your every move for clues and indeed, you are carefully assessing them.

Often the students with challenging behaviour will not misbehave at first but will watch quietly as they work out what they can get away with.

Another word of caution. Don't try to overload them with too many rules and regulations. That in itself can cause unnecessary tension. You can introduce the most important rules but try to get on with some work as soon as possible. Do not spend half the lesson lecturing them as to what is and what is not acceptable.

Make sure that the work is pitched so that everyone can get on with it. The function of the work in the first lesson is really to get them started and see how the dynamics of the group start to operate.

Be relaxed but above all aim for a slightly formal approach with the attitude of a typical teacher who has been doing this many times. That way you can assess the class over the first few lessons before you decide on specific approaches.

One of the most useful ways to spend your time as a teacher is to observe other experienced teachers' lessons. It is a surprising thing that after most teachers qualify they often complain that they don't have enough time to observe other teachers. There is also an underlying feeling that the training and the observing phase is over and there is a desire to get on and just do it.

Another thing is that in a busy week it takes quite a strong will to give up a free period to observe another teacher. There is yet another problem. Often you feel that rather than just observe, maybe you should be helping out a bit, especially if the class is demanding.

Despite all of this, I can't stress enough how valuable observing other teachers is. This is particularly so if there are a range of teachers and subjects that you can observe regularly over a period of time. When you ask them, make it clear that you respect them as teachers and want to learn from them. Importantly, at the end of the lesson, point out some specific things which you have learnt from them and I find that this becomes a great confidence booster to the observed teacher.

You will be amazed at how much you learn from an experienced teacher. Although I have been teaching for nearly two decades I take every opportunity I can to look in and observe other teachers. If you think about it, if you regularly observe say, five teachers and they have an average teaching experience of 20 years each, then you are making immediately available a resource of a whole century of skill!

Particularly look at how they deal with challenging students. I can promise you that if you find the will and the time to do this, you will wonder why every teacher doesn't do it. The best thing is that you can put the ideas you learn into practise immediately and experience the benefits straight away.

When you are explaining the task to the whole group and organizing the transition for them to start the task or activity you will find that this is an area where a particular problem can creep in.

From observing many lessons I know that a specific behaviour problem at this stage is caused because many students don't know exactly what to do. This is because they often weren't listening to the instructions (even though they may have looked like they were!)

In response to this I have seen teachers go round and explain individually what to do to 30 students. That is obviously a ridiculous situation to get into.

Also, many students sense that a significant amount of students don't know what to do and use this feeling of unease to help them get out of doing any work because: 'I don't get it! Nobody gets it!'

It is natural for a teacher to say things like: 'Why didn't you listen when I was explaining to the whole class?', but this is not helpful.

A good way to help solve this problem, or rather prevent it from happening, is to use 'specific examples'. You can use this technique immediately to great effect.

This is what you do. You refer to problems that have commonly happened before. For example: 'When I did this last year a lot of students got confused. They didn't realize that the information is all on this green sheet. It's all mixed up and you have to sort it out and write it in the correct boxes on the pink sheet.' This method takes away the confrontational aspect and makes it more interesting to the students.

It reinforces what they have to do and sets in motion a subconscious challenge that they won't make the mistake that the other group did.

IMMEDIATELY CHANGE HOW YOU PLAN

Most teachers naturally plan their lessons in accordance with the syllabus. They start off with what is needed to be taught and break it down into tasks and activities. Behaviour management then becomes something which is bolted on or adjusted as the work is taught and as difficulties arise.

When you deal with students with challenging behaviour you should turn the planning system on its head. You should start by thinking through how your particular students deal with activities. What works well for them? What sorts of safe stuff could you do to start the lesson going? What do they have trouble with? How can you minimize disruption? How can you arrange a smooth flow? Think, in detail about how those students actually, in reality deal with those tasks.

For example, if you have an idea to get students to match cards up with each other, have you really thought out carefully what this means? Will the leaving of seats cause trouble? Have you got a plan B you could quickly switch to? Would it be better not to have cards at all but rather to have all they need in one place on one carefully designed worksheet?

By changing the way you think about planning, you will immediately improve the chances of how the work is done. Of course you have to keep the syllabus materials as the core but the process becomes different. What can they already do? – followed by how can these new materials be fitted to what they can do?

When you get into the habit of thinking this way, you set up a whole new way of working. It saves untold trouble. Obviously, as you become more experienced you become more skilled at doing this. But not always. I have observed teachers who have taught for many years and still are 'content' centred rather than 'process' centred. It just shows how powerful habits can be.

This idea works straight away and is very effective for helping with great behaviour management.

You create a 'class vision'. You ask the class for their help in building a mental picture of what things will look like, in detail, by the end of the lesson.

For example you might say: 'By the end of this lesson we will have four of you seated around this table, having an imaginary dinner and speaking to each other in French. One of you will be a waiter and will write the order in this small notebook. Others will be the objects around the room, standing nice and still. One of you, for instance, might be a lovely potted plant and say in French: 'I am a pretty little plant'. One of you might be a succulent joint of roast beef and say, in French: 'Can you smell me, I'm a lovely beef joint?' There will be lots of other things for the rest of you to be.'

It helps if you can move around the room and indicate with your hands enthusiastically where things will be. Importantly, you then you say: 'But to achieve this, what have we got to do? How can we make sure only one person speaks at a time?' The students will suggest basic rules of behaviour management back to you and you can say: 'That's right Abigail, if only one person speaks at a time we'll have a calm order and we'll get there! Well done.'

The vision of what you want the class to achieve and how you're going to get there magically fuses together the content of the lesson and the reasons why good behaviour is essential. What's more, because the class helps you contribute to the vision, there is more chance of them keeping to the behaviour that they themselves have suggested.

THE INSTANT POWER OF THE REPORT

Supposing you have a new class and a serious problem rapidly develops.

For example, say a student is being picked on by several of the others and nasty comments are being made. It may well be hard to establish how many are involved.

You give your usual warnings and use your normal behaviour strategies but they don't seem to be having that much effect.

So what do you do? I have found that you can use 'The Instant Power of the Report.' You have with you some official looking prepared headed paper. At the top it will say in bold print: 'REPORT TO HEAD TEACHER FOR SERIOUS CONCERN'.

You make sure that the class has some work to be getting on with. You then work your way round, purportedly helping students in various parts of the room. You then quietly have little chats with the main students who were making the nasty comments.

You say, in a hushed voice, something like: 'Hallo Anthony. I know we don't know each other yet. I'm afraid there's a little bit of a problem here. You know you were shouting out those horrible things at Jason, and you know when I kept asking you to stop you ignored me? Well, the problem I've got is that the Head Teacher absolutely insists we make a full report about something as serious as this. Obviously I'll have to go to his office straight after this lesson.' You then show him the report, write his name clearly on it and then say: 'I have to put a reason on here. Can you tell me why it was you ignored me?'

Now at this point the student will deny, or say it wasn't just him. You tell him not to worry, in a matter of fact way. You explain that you will be speaking to everyone concerned.

Interestingly, if you bring full attention back to the lesson, and mention that you'll do the report later, then the problem can often disappear!

When faced with students who are very challenging in their behaviour it is very important to carefully manage the conversations you have with them.

Students who are used to getting into trouble expect a certain approach from a teacher. They have often become quite immune to being told off. In many cases they are severely told off at home and may well have been subjected to violence.

The key to dealing with such students is to build up long term and trusting relationships. But if you need a technique which has immediate effect, then try the following:

First of all, surprise them with your response. I have seen teachers go in full throttle and of course this escalates the temperature of the situation.

I have also seen teachers go in with a soft gentle approach but with many students you can sense that the student is thinking: 'Ah . . . the soft gentle approach. We can have some fun here.' I've seen students cleverly making fun of the teacher and the teacher is unaware.

I have developed an approach which I call in my training sessions: 'The strategic deflective conversation'. It works like this. You engage the student in conversation which has got nothing to do with the behaviour issue. The function of this is to establish a bit of common ground. It allows the relationship between you to settle and be a bit more comfortable.

You then mention, in an oblique way, the behaviour issue. So you might say: 'I saw you getting a bit bored just earlier. Chucking paper planes around is a sign of boredom, isn't it? I tell you what, I'll try and make the next bit a little bit more interesting, but could you do your bit? Could you not throw anymore planes?' Give a smile, and create that adult to adult sense of expectancy and move away and get on with the lesson.

STRATEGIC DEFLECTIVE CONVERSATIONS

Although this idea can take a long time, once you put it in place and start using it the tremendous effects can be felt immediately.

You involve the students continually in your own behaviour management improvement programme.

How you select and give feedback on the improvements to the students is vitally important. You might say: 'Listen class. Someone was annoyed last lesson because they got told off for leaving their seat. All they wanted to do was sharpen a pencil. Well, I've got a solution. Look, I've got these sharpeners where the waste goes into the unit so there's no need to leave your seat.'

Or an example might be: 'You know you said the noise levels got too loud last lesson and many of you couldn't work? Well, look, let's use this as a solution to the problem (show the noise level symbol card). As soon as you see this if everyone cooperates we'll all be happy. Thank you!'

It is a way of explaining the problem and not so much using rules but rather solutions that the class can come up with together.

If they complained about being too hot, despite the windows being open, for example you might say: 'Look, Michael suggested this as a solution: (hold up a door wedge) I'm going to wedge open the door to let the air flow through. We'll have to be extra quiet though . . .'

The method has the advantage that instead of the teacher continually imposing rules on the students the situation is looked at as: 'How can we as a group solve these problems together?'

The students love the idea that they have a say, within reason. The teacher might say: 'Christine said I talked too long last time. I'll keep it shorter today, but, of course, there're certain things I must tell you, so listen extra well.'

Although this idea takes a little bit of planning and preparation, it can be put into use immediately with a new group and you will see its results straight away.

It is based on the deep desire we all have to collect full sets. How many of us remember frantic trade-offs when we were at school, when we tried so hard to collect a full set of, say, football cards?

The power of this phenomenon can be utilized in the management of behaviour.

You prepare a large chart for your class and type out the names and several columns. You then prepare a set of stickers. Make sure that each category is a different colour. So for example, arriving on time might be green; not calling out could be blue; working hard will be perhaps red and so on. You identify the key behaviour areas you want to concentrate on.

An important point for this idea to work well is to not give out the stickers too easily. It may be, for example, that the student has to be on time for every lesson for a week to get the green sticker. However, once you have established your own reasonable conditions you can start sticking them on the chart against the students' names.

The chart becomes a powerful negotiating tool. It is incredible how a student, seeing that they need a yellow sticker to complete a set, will work extra hard to achieve it. Once a full set has been achieved a certificate can be proudly awarded and a new set begun.

The beauty is that the chart is permanently visible and works on the subconscious of the students. They really are keen to 'collect' full sets. The flexibility of the idea is that you can fine-tune and design the stickers to match the requirements of the group.

A problem I have often observed is the strange fact that a small percentage of students can skilfully command a huge proportion of the teacher's time. The teacher attends to the ever urgent needs of the few but unfortunately the needs of the many are left neglected.

I have discovered that a simple worksheet and a firm and clear explanation can have an immediate effect in helping to solve this age-old problem. You explain clearly, from the outset, to the class that you want to be able to go round and see everyone work. That is only fair.

You prepare a sheet headed: 'Waiting for the teacher sheet' and on it you include a variety of small activities. The function of the sheet is to occupy the student while you help others.

The selection of contents for the sheet is important. I find the following examples work well:

1. A box where the student can write questions about what he doesn't understand.
2. A small word search.
3. An outline of a picture to be coloured in (provide two colours)
4. A small simple drawing with a box to copy it.
5. A set of straightforward general knowledge questions.
6. A personal question: 'What have you done in the last year which you're pleased with?'
7. A favourites section: favourite food; colour; number and so on.
8. A few simple maths problems.

You can of course adapt the sheet depending on the type of group.

You say to the student: 'Look, I can't see you straight away and I know you need help. Could you just have a go at this sheet which is especially designed to exercise different parts of your mind. I will be back as soon as I can.' Then attend to other students in the room.

You will find that the sheet holds the interest of the challenging few and automatically helps improve the behaviour of the class.

Building Longer Term Strategies

Find out who, in your school, is serious about improving their craft at behaviour management. Suggest starting a weekly club after school and meet for about half an hour. If it is longer than that people tend to get put off. If it is less frequent than weekly, it can lose its momentum. I find that Fridays after school is best.

In the club sessions discuss behaviour management situations which you encounter everyday and seek advice from each other on the best way of dealing with them. Exchange ideas in a friendly humorous way. Appoint a club leader or be one yourself.

Keep it simple and straight forward. Do not have minutes or paper work or charts or statistics. Just meet and chat. A classroom is the best venue as you can role play situations for discussion. There are role plays in Section 8 of this book which you may wish to use as part of your training.

Over time you will find that the sharing of knowledge removes that feeling of isolation, characteristic of the teaching experience. You will get that reassuring feeling that it is not just you who has trouble and faces challenges . It helps you to see behaviour management as a key part of the job you do. Regularly hearing others' experiences will give you a more balanced sense of perspective.

It will refocus away from staffroom moaning routines to a shared desire to look at solutions, try out ideas and report back next week. A buzz will be created and more and more will join. A feeling of teamwork and shared problems will emerge. Congratulate each other as good outcomes are reported back. Analyse situations where things go wrong. Always have a collective club attitude of 'how could we do this better next time?'

I highly recommend you starting up and continuing with a 'Behaviour Management Club'.

THE BEHAVIOUR MANAGEMENT CLUB

One of the most effective strategies I use with challenging behaviour is sheer persistence and resilience. When you teach a lesson, you naturally have an overall structure and plan in mind. Good teachers know that they have to be adaptable and flexible to mould their plan as required. It is a huge bonus when you can arrange to give students choices of what they do and of how they do it. But you have to be careful. I have seen teachers be so flexible that the strong minded students are able to argue at every point about what they should be doing. Once the teacher gives in, then it is doubly hard for him to put his foot down next time.

The secret is to show a certain flexibility within the structure of what it is you want to teach them. When you are challenged about an important piece of work with comments like: 'Can we not do this . . . it's boring. Why can't we get straight on to the so and so,' you must reply, with firm quiet and determined persistence, that the piece of work is certainly necessary and you persist in how you persuade them to do it. Keep on and they will then know that the plan you have is more or less the plan you will always follow.

Work set will never be to the liking of the whole class. It is tempting for a teacher to bend and then bend again his lesson plan in an effort to appease a disgruntled student but you must be careful not to allow the more vocal members of the group to control what material is actually taught. Your responsibility is to deliver the scheme of work to the whole class. With careful and determined use of persistence you will find that there will be less and less challenges to the tasks you ask them to do.

Much advice given about behaviour management speaks of modelling behaviour designed for your students to emulate. The belief is that students who don't know how to act appropriately will observe teachers who turn up on time, stay calm and speak politely and become changed citizens. I don't deny that these qualities are important and they, in fact, form the backbone of my teaching strategies, but to think that this alone will affect change is to be deluded.

The challenging students you face have been exposed from infancy to an ocean of influences from different sources. Can we really expect students who can hardly read, have damaged backgrounds, low self-esteem, and who regularly use aggression to cover their lack of confidence to imbibe this model of behaviour and change? At best, all we can hope to represent is a mere drop in their ocean of influence. Some teachers believe that the typically poorly behaved student would see the well dressed, calm, smiling teacher as a model to emulate. This is because the teacher is mistakenly grafting his own aspirations onto the ideal aspirations of the students.

In my opinion, based on teaching thousands of challenging students, teachers would do better by modelling the behaviour of experienced teachers who are skilled in the craft of behaviour management. Our goal is to maintain a calm class full of challenging students and create situations where good learning can take place. All our strategies are designed to that end.

When I now meet some of the most difficult students I have taught, I don't think they ever really modelled their lives on my behaviour or ever will. But I can tell from the warmth I often feel from them, that what they respect me for is the invisible skill that I managed to use to make their classroom experience, as productive and as enjoyable as I possibly could, bearing in mind all the difficulties we all had to deal with at the time.

In summary, don't get too hung up on behaving in a way which you hope they will emulate. Instead, focus your energies on the mastery of classroom craft. That is what really counts in the end.

WILL THEY REALLY MODEL YOUR BEHAVIOUR?

IDEA
54

When I was training, the best teacher I ever had the privilege to watch was a man named Bob. At the time he was well into his 60s and he still teaches today even though he is well into his 80s. He seemed to have a magic way of handling the students. He always taught the most challenging ones and they loved him. One day I asked him: 'What is the secret?' The answer he gave, I shall always cherish. 'They know,' he said, 'they know, deep down inside, if you care or not. You've got to show you care about them!'

But how do you show your care?

What has worked for me is that you show care in thousands of little ways and importantly, you show that care, regardless of how they treat you. That may sound impossible, but it works for me. Over a period of time they feel what you're trying to do and they respond in a gradual but profound way.

You may ask them how their sick nan is, as they are leaving the room. You may show a concern if they are thirsty. You may hand them a tissue if they wish to blow their nose. There are thousands of examples. You take the time to show care in those little ways and it becomes built into you as part of the way you do business as a teacher.

And there is another thing too, and I am prepared to offer a guarantee for this. A teacher who cares and takes an interest in their students as part of the way they do business and despite how their students treat them, will win them over in the end. It may take time, but as long as their other behaviour management techniques are sound, they will win them over as sure as night follows day.

I commend Bob's advice to you. Show them you care!

This idea and the use of it has helped many from quitting the teaching profession. I have found that in my training of new teachers, this particular idea has touched a deep nerve.

The main problem when dealing with challenging behaviour is to keep yourself mentally resilient and strong. It is the anxiety of the feeling of endless hurdles to jump which helps tire out teachers. It has been said many times that the total workload of a teacher can often feel overwhelming. Sometimes with tackling challenging behaviour, each new day can begin to seem more and more daunting.

Most teachers feel that however hard they work, however many hours they do, there remains an endless stream of worrying tasks still unfinished. The exhaustion that starts to set in lowers their ability to deal with the challenges.

The technique I recommend is very simple. Whatever you are doing, remember to remove the mental strain by thinking 100 per cent about what is going on at that moment. Cast out from your mind the unfinished tasks. Bring all your attention to bear on the moment. Notice the little details.

With practise, and it does take a lot of practise, you can make this technique a working habit. You will realize that a lot of things you do today will have to be repeated tomorrow and it is pointless to do them with any sense of strain. Just take one thing at a time and concentrate all your attention on that one thing. Cultivate a kind of working relaxation and you will be investing in long term success and happiness as a teacher.

Many know of this technique but few actually use it. Be one of those who use it regularly and notice how much better you will feel. Your renewed relaxed and centred presence in itself will greatly enhance your management of behaviour.

HELP THEM GET WHAT THEY WANT

One of the best ways to manage behaviour with challenging students is to build up good strong teaching relationships. But how do you do that?

In my book *100+ Ideas for Managing Behaviour* I discuss 'Using Their Life Targets to Motivate'. I've found that over time this idea can be wonderfully developed. You can keep a separate book with the bold heading which says: 'Students' Ambitions'.

As you chat with the students individually find out what it is they want to achieve in life. This will take time and patience as many of them will profess to having no ambitions at all. But probing a little can reveal all sorts of ambitions. I've found that the main barrier can be their own confidence in believing they can achieve. A teacher can never be better than when she is helping a student achieve her ambitions.

It is a good idea to just check with the student and say: 'Is it OK if I find out a few things about what you want to do to try and help you get there?'

It is a simple system. You have a page headed with the student's name and you jot down notes about what they want and how they might achieve it. You can find out about courses on offer and perhaps arrange a meeting with people who already do what the student wants to do. You can find out from career guides what the skills and requirements are. You can note down what the potential obstacles and difficulties might be. Importantly you can jot down notes about how to get round those obstacles.

You can enthusiastically share the information with them from time to time. Just short comments here and there work much better than long meetings.

The fact that you are actively trying to help them achieve what they want will be one of the ways you can really help build a good relationship in the long term.

One of the most devastating behaviours for disrupting a class is ongoing conflicts between students. You can carry out a lot of superficial work like separating them in the room, isolating one of them to another classroom and putting them on all sorts of reports. You can also refer them to the relevant pastoral team. But if the problem rumbles on over a series of lessons I have found great advantage in trying the following.

You arrange an appointment to see the two of them after school. You listen to both sides of the problem. You may find that the conflict is deeply entrenched back to the last school they were at together. There can, of course, be a huge amount of reasons. Maybe they just can't stand each other.

You then set them a challenge. You explain that all through life we have to work with people whom we don't necessarily like. Give animated examples from your own life where you had to find a way to get on with someone whom you didn't like (never give actual names). Explain that we simply have to find ways of getting on with each other. You then say: 'If you two can work in my next lesson without trouble I will be extremely pleased with you both because I know that is a really hard thing to do. I'm not expecting you to become best friends. All I want you to do is tolerate each other peacefully. Do you think you could do that?'

You will be surprised that by taking an active and direct interest and setting them a specific challenge they will try to improve the situation. In the next lesson be sure to thank them if things are even slightly better.

Your reputation will also get round that you are a teacher who tries to solve problems. You may not always succeed, but it is the fact that you try that will gradually endear you to the students.

WHEN A STUDENT IS IN ISOLATION

There will be times when you are asked to provide 'isolation work' for a student who has been isolated from your lesson. It maybe that she was involved in some sort of trouble in another lesson.

It is my experience that you have normally just got your class quiet when the door opens and someone asks for isolation work. Therefore, make sure that you have a supply of ready-made isolation work at your finger tips so that you can pass it on at a moment's notice and not be distracted from your lesson.

A really important advantage can be made here if you recognize the opportunity. It is usual that the students isolated from your lessons are normally extremely poorly behaved. Make a point of tracking them down to find out where they are working in isolation so that you can chat to them and make sure that they understand the work. It is a great opportunity to help build the relationship on a one to one basis, removed from the stress of the classroom and with an attitude of helpfulness rather than conflict.

You can ask them what the trouble is and why they have been isolated. You can listen with interest and understanding. It is an excellent idea to, at that point, remind the student of the things you are really happy about in your lessons and say what a shame it is that this little bit of trouble has kept them out of a few lessons.

The interesting thing is that even really badly behaved students would be feeling a bit deflated by the situation and the timing of having a teacher come and say encouraging words and look forward to next time they come into the lesson is an investment which will pay huge dividends.

If you are a stickler for every rule and follow up everything to the letter of the law and never waiver under the impression that you see yourself as a consistent teacher, then I can tell you for certain that you will wear yourself out, become unpopular and be known as inflexible. Your behaviour management will not necessarily be good.

If, on the other hand, you let students off things far too much and do not consistently apply the rules then you will be seen by other teachers as letting the system down. You will be seen as a soft touch by your students and they will soon form the impression that they can get away with anything. Your behaviour management will be poor.

I use 'intelligent compromises'. What does this mean? Let's take an example. Supposing Rachel arrives at your lesson still eating her sandwich from break. If you are a stickler you would demand that she stop eating and either put the food away or throw it in the bin immediately. You would enforce that decision with everything at your disposal.

If you were a softie you might let her eat it in the lesson. But, for this situation, and countless like it, I would deploy an 'intelligent compromise'. The key thing with this approach is that it involves judgement. I might let her spend a minute outside the room finishing it off and then have a word at the end of the lesson to explain that I wouldn't be able to do that again, because of the rules.

It may be that she had no breakfast and was delayed from the last class and ended up in the back of the queue.

The point of the 'intelligent compromise' is that it encourages cooperation from your students because they see that you are applying the rules in a fair way.

To last in the long run always try to use the 'intelligent compromise'.

INTELLIGENT COMPROMISE

THE BEST SUPPORT YOU CAN EVER GET

The best support you will ever get is from the student's home. In reality most teachers only speak to the parents and guardians at parents' evenings. Even then a great many of the parents you would like to see don't turn up.

Also, when teachers phone home it is often because something has gone wrong.

The best way to build support networks with the more challenging students is to have short, brief and regular contact via a variety of methods, the whole year round.

In practice a busy teacher will find it hard to find the time to phone home and have long drawn out conversations. But there is a better way.

Try to set up two way messages which are short, specific and regular. For example, write a little note to the parent asking what she thinks of a particular piece of work. Check with the student to show the work and look out for the reply. Just a few scribbled words of reply works wonders for communication.

Have ready printed notes where you can jot in a few words of praise for specific work down. Have a supply of envelopes and write the parent's name and seal up the envelope and ask the student to deliver it. Include a folded envelop with your name written on it for a reply. This gives the note more status and is more likely to get a reply. When you speak to the student about their work and refer to the notes from home it gives the whole thing more meaning.

Importantly, if you have been having some sort of regular contact, based on praise, if the time comes to ask for their support with a behaviour issue you are much more likely to get a successful outcome.

Common Dangers and How to Avoid Them

Imagine the following. You are starting a lesson and just prior to the lesson maybe there has been a fire drill or maybe there has been a fight. There can be lots of reasons but the point is that the students arrive in an unsettled state.

You allow them settling down time but unfortunately, a significant chunk of the group will not settle. There can well be a whole variety of unsettled behaviour but the effect can be very difficult for the teacher. The temptation is to act strongly because all other options have been tried. The problem is that your annoyance will feed more energy into a whirlpool of unsettled energy.

Rather than get annoyed, the idea here is to do the exact opposite. Stay calm and stay still. Say nothing. Just adopt an uncharacteristic silence but importantly adopt a strong posture and a facial expression of a firm calm disapproval. Wait. Do not be tempted to say or do anything. The students know that they have pushed you too far and there is a certain power in your stillness and silence.

The waiting allows the energy in the room to drain away a little. The students are not quite sure what you are going to do next and that is what gives this technique its power. You wait until things settle down and then in a calm voice you say: 'I have waited for you. I have prepared this lesson and I am trying to teach it. I do realize that something has unsettled you. But enough is enough. You've gone too far now!' Then continue with your lesson.

As always try to get them actually working on something as quickly as possible and if some individuals ignore your instructions you must take the next step, which may mean removing them. The point is that you will find, with this technique, that in most cases it helps to turn the situation round without having to remove people.

THE SLOW MOTION BUTTON

Have a 'slow motion button' in your mind. This is the metaphorical button in your imagination (visualize it as say a bright wooden yellow button, and when you press it a soft sound of birdsong emits and the lighting changes to yellow) which you can press when the heat is on. Challenging situations in classrooms can develop rapidly and from out of nowhere. The teacher's instinctive reaction, although natural, surprisingly can contribute to the problems which start to escalate.

Here's an example: a teacher was asking a student why he was messing about in her science lesson and the student quite aggressively tore up the carefully prepared colour worksheet and said 'You are a useless teacher and this is a useless lesson!' The teacher felt quite put out after the late night of preparation that she had the night before and, getting to the end of her patience with this student instinctively replied: 'We'll you're a useless student if you rip up my resources like that!'

The student then pushed a chair at her, hurting her legs and ran out of the room shouting 'I'm going to tell my dad you said I was useless! He'll have you!'

If only she had pushed the 'Slow Motion Button'! When you push this button you deliberately slow everything down which allows you time to consider the situation and think about your response. You allow yourself a bit of space to view the situation from a distance. It is important to note that when you use this idea as a habit, the provocative behaviour can be actually used as a trigger to push the button. You will find that it will give you those vital few moments of thought time and restore to you control in the midst of the stress. It will help prevent you from rashly reacting and will save you no end of trouble.

Some students have found that a great way of getting out of doing any work and at the same time having a bit of fun by getting the teacher in a 'tizzy', is to repeat in various ways that they simply don't understand how to do the work.

Of course there will obviously be countless times when, despite your best efforts, the student genuinely doesn't understand.

A big part of knowing whether the behaviour is genuine or not can depend on how well you know the student. But it isn't always easy to work out exactly what is going on.

The key thing is to have ready a process. The student will sometimes try to make you feel bad with such comments as: 'Mrs Green explains it better than you do.'

Remain calm, as always. Explain that you have had a lot of experience with this and it is quite natural to have trouble understanding new work. Have ready a set of step by step simplified worksheets that break the task into smaller tasks. Also have a set of easy tasks which relate to the main task but are also much easier to do as preparation. In an encouraging way explain the easier task and ask them to have a go and then give them space to get on with it, making it clear that you will be back soon to help.

If the student immediately complains that they don't get it, or adds in another problem, like 'this is boring', then you can be sure that the student was using that technique to get out of working.

This is where you must become firmer. Reassure them that once they start working they will be fine, and further encourage them, by a quick reference back, to some of their previous work.

You will find that in the majority of cases applying this process quietly and with determination will solve the problem.

THE WHOLE CLASS JUST CAN'T BE BOTHERED

Sometimes you find that the whole class just can't be bothered and are pleading to do something fun. Maybe they are too hot, or tired after an exam, or harassed after some disruption to the normal routine. The list goes on.

The temptation to abandon the lesson and let them do something 'fun' at such times is very strong and I have known many colleagues (including myself) to give in to this. They feel that it would be easier to let them do something 'fun' rather than to battle on against all odds with the lesson plan.

But it is always a mistake to do this. For one thing, it will quickly deteriorate into chaos. Students will argue with each other about what fun activity to do and if, for example, you gave out some board games, you would very soon be faced with a whole range of disorder issues. Not only that, but they will lose a lesson.

But to battle on with your planned lesson will cause all sorts of problems too. So what do you do? I have discovered that you can effectively use a bargaining technique.

This is how it works. You explain to them briefly what the planned lesson was to be and why it is important. You then say that because it is so hot (or whatever the reason is) you are happy to agree to a shorter, easier lesson with a fun activity at the end, if the objectives of the shorter lesson are more or less met.

This shows you to be flexible and reasonable. Most students then go along with this.

You will have prepared a shorter version in advance and you will find that quite a bit gets done using this technique. Everybody loves a bargain and the students feel that they are getting out of doing some of the work and therefore are compliant because they have an advantage over a normal lesson.

Students calling out when you are trying to speak to the whole class is one of the most common and disruptive things a teacher has to deal with.

I have found that the best way to deal with it in the vast majority of cases is to keep your instructions running at a brisk pace and respond to the calling out in a certain way, rather than stopping the flow and showing annoyance. If you stop what you're saying and tell the student off in a harsh way, it changes the chemistry and mood of the class, the momentum is lost and it invites further calling out (because they are entertained by your reactions).

By being upbeat you keep the mood right but be careful. You don't want to encourage others to call out so your response must be of a particular type. You say (quickly): 'It's great that you've got some ideas, I do want to hear them, but please wait. Let me finish talking to the whole class first.' If that particular student calls out again, repeat the words, slightly firmer, hold a slightly sterner look and reinforce it with a hand block, but keep the pace upbeat and going forward.

Sometimes, and interestingly, by increasing the speed of what you say the class listens better. There are times when it is right to stop in mid-sentence and glare at the interrupter, but as a rule, really try to keep the pace going and reduce the interrupters to insignificance with swift, appropriate comments.

Also, make sure that you keep what you are saying very short and tell them that. You can always break down what you are going to tell them into chunks delivered through the course of the lesson. It is surprising how so many teachers try to explain everything at the start. It is better to keep to one clear and quickly delivered instruction at a time.

DRAWING ON DESKS

Quite a common problem is students who draw on desks. Very often it is not noticed until the class has left the room. It is very hard to find out and prove which student did it after the event. The ink on the desk creates a very poor impression with your next class and can often lead to complaints from the next student who has to sit there and get ink all over their hands and work.

There is a very simple preventative solution to add to your daily checklist of reminders as part of your teaching routine.

When your class has sat down, just walk down the rows and point out that all the desk tops are nice and clean and you would like them to stay that way. Briefly mention that you will have a look at the end of the lesson and each student is of course responsible to keep their own desk nice and clean.

Don't forget to make a thing of looking round at the end of the lesson to check that desks are ok.

If you find a bit of writing on a desk at the end, it is my experience that the student will deny it was him. It is important to refer the matter to your line manager which sends a message to the class that you are bothered about damage to the desks. The students will generally be bothered about things which you are bothered about.

If you find the desks OK then be sure to thank them for keeping their desks clean.

By being conscientious about this helps improve standards in lots of areas, for example scribbling in exercise books, because it shows that you care and will follow things up.

One of the most common problems for teachers is holding the attention of the whole class to give instructions. With some challenging classes this can become a running battle. You can try all sorts of things like getting senior teachers in and taking people out of the room and a whole host of other things but sometimes a significant restless core of students simply persist in not listening.

A good strategy is to use a two-tier system. This is how it works. You keep your instructions to the whole class to a very short time in order to set them up with a task to be getting on with. The class get used to knowing that this will be a short snappy session.

Then, when the whole class is getting on with their work, you speak to one quarter of the class in turn, where you can offer more detailed instructions. A good way to do it is to designate an area of the classroom for each of the four groups. You gather them round you and give more detailed instructions. You position yourself so that you can watch the rest of the class at the same time. You then get them to sit down and carry on and you gather round your next group in another part of the classroom.

The advantage of this strategy is that it takes the strain away from the initial presentation at the start and it allows for more relaxed and efficient small sessions of teaching. A lot of students feel more comfortable in asking questions about the work in smaller groups. It also discourages the 'court jesters' from playing to the gallery as the audience for them becomes a small group rather than the whole class.

This strategy should not be used instead of whole class instructions but as an optional and extremely useful, supplement to it.

TWO TIER WHOLE CLASS LISTENING

One of the most common dangers in behaviour management is the amount of students who don't pay attention and the considerable chain reaction of disruption which then arises.

For many students it seems that the lesson is something they just have to somehow survive. When they don't pay attention, they, then, obviously don't know what to do. It becomes an excessive drain on you to have to keep going round explaining what they should have listened to. Also, they can become easily involved in low level disruption to amuse themselves and ward off boredom.

There is, of course, no one golden way of making students pay attention. A lot of the techniques in this book aim at ways of trying to engage attention. Indeed, a huge part of a teacher's job is to develop ways of getting students' attention.

However, I have found that one thing is especially useful in getting attention. It is to do with how our minds work. Many teachers talk in the abstract or refer to non-specific ideas or general things. It is very hard for the mind to latch onto vague things.

Try to be specific in the details of what you say. Try to make the details vivid, dramatic and full of action. They have more impact that way.

For example, supposing you were talking about Newton and Gravity. You could outline his theory of gravity in a dull, flat, factual way or you could get them to imagine a huge bright green apple, with a little worm in it, falling out of the tree and thumping him on the head. You could describe the bruise on his head. Purple and yellow and sore! Do an impression of him looking up. Suddenly he has a thought: 'Gravity'!

With creative imagination you can bring everything you say to life by using vivid details. By gaining and holding your students' attention you will automatically cut down on a lot of the common behaviour problems.

I am amazed how commonly behaviour management problems occur because a teacher has been slack with their management of time.

Take the case of starting a class when 10 minutes in, half a dozen students arrive flustered because 'the bell went in PE when we were still out on the field!'

Time can be your best friend for dealing with the management of behaviour. Or, to put it more accurately, the way you use time to control activities, can be your best friend.

When you ask students to come to the front to demonstrate something, by having a strict time allowance, for example: 'We only have one minute for this one' produces brisk pace and structured order.

When you set a starter and say: 'Right 4 minutes please. On your marks, get set, go!' It creates urgency and focuses attention. It discourages misbehaviour.

When you go to individuals who are not working and make a little mark a few lines down and say: 'I'll be back in 7 minutes, and I want you to have written up at least to there please', you have made a specific time goal and it motivates wonderfully.

If you have planned well in advance, by keeping a close eye on the time, the organized collecting in of materials, then you will have time for a good plenary at the end without that awful sense of rushing.

By writing a basic lesson plan on the board and ticking off the activities against the time as the lesson progresses you help create a sense of urgency and importance for what needs to be done. Talking about the activity and the time allocated gives a feel of authority. It powerfully encourages compliance.

Be conscious of your detailed use of time and you will find that it becomes your friend and automatically removes many of the problems commonly seen in behaviour management.

TAKING EACH OTHER'S PROPERTY

One of the very common problems you encounter in a classroom which seems to cause disproportionate trouble and often leads to complaints from parents is when students interfere with and take each others' property.

Students might think it amusing, for example, to hide someone's bag. But all hell can break loose over things like this.

I have tried many techniques to deal with this problem over the years and I have found the following to be the most effective.

At the very first signs that anybody is interfering with anybody else's property you stop the lesson and make a big thing of it with an announcement like:

'I would like you all to put down your pens and listen carefully to what I have to say. (long pause, insist on silence). Now I know that nobody in here would take or intentionally damage someone else's property. (pause, create serious atmosphere and look round the class) But it seems that a few of you are being a bit silly and starting to mess about with others' property for a joke. Now I must warn you that if I see anyone interfere with anyone else's stuff I will write down their name immediately. I'm not going to get into arguments about it now. If there is a complaint about any property going missing or being damaged in this lesson then you will have to explain why, despite this very clear warning, you continued to do what you did. But it won't be me you speak to. It will be to the senior staff! I will have no choice but to refer this. I hope I have made myself clear and I now want to get on with some good work.'

You then continue with your lesson but keep extra vigilance for any signs of trouble in this area.

Getting to the Heart of Problems through Role Plays

8

Scenario: The teacher has settled the class, with some difficulty, and a student arrives very late for the lesson.

Problem Focus: How to deal with a latecomer.

Characters: A = student who arrives late; B = another student already in the classroom; C = teacher.

Role Play

A: (comes into the room late, after the teacher has settled the class) Did you see the fight? Good weren't it? (laughing and calling across to his friends in the class and displaying total disregard for the teacher's authority).

C: You're late (rising voice) again! That's twice this week!

A: I can't help it, it's no good you shouting at me – the teachers round the fight wanted us to tell them what we saw.

C: I don't care about that (intending to make a firm example of him in front of the class). I've started my lesson and you've ruined it. How dare you come in like that?

B: Sir, he couldn't help it!

C: Now don't you join in, be quiet!

B: But it's not fair!

A: He gave him a right good smack, I'll tell yer! It was great!

B: Where is he now?

A: They took him off to the . . .

C: (shouting) I've had enough of this. You two, shut up now or get out !

(The two students get up and prance out of the room explaining in a loud voice that they intend to tell the head of year about how unfair the teacher is . . . .)

Points for Reflection and Discussion:

1. Notice how the teacher's rising anger escalates the problems. How else could it be handled?
2. Try working on Version 2 which is role play 72 and then compare results and outcomes.

Scenario: The teacher has settled the class and a student arrives late for the lesson.

Problem Focus: How to deal with a latecomer.

Characters: A = student who arrives late; B = another student already in the classroom; C = teacher.

Role Play

A: Did you see the fight? Good weren't it ? (laughing and calling across to his friends in the class).

C: (stands still) Could you sit down please, Stephen. I can see you've been caught up in something, we'll have a little chat later. Thank you. That's good (turns to the class and resumes, confidently expecting attention). Now class, as I say, copy the numbers into the boxes and then . . .

A: You should have seen his face

B: Was it a mess?

A: Yes, it was . . . (other students get distracted).

C: Stephen, I can see you want to talk about this, but if you could just hold on a few moments please, let me finish what I was saying to the class and then I'll come over to you. (hold the pause, cue the class and use a firm but friendly look) Now class, copy the numbers into the boxes and . . . (friendly positive tone in voice).

A: I knew they'd make something of it . . .

C: (hand block and slightly firmer tone) That's quite enough Stephen, come on, I must finish this (firm look towards Stephen for a few moments).

A: Sorry.

C: Thank you. Now, as I say, copy the numbers into the boxes and then . . . .

Points for Reflection and Discussion:

Notice how positive language and friendly tone stop the situation from escalating. In Version 1 the teacher loses control. What the teacher said inflamed the situation. In Version 2 the teacher kept control, and managed the control without losing authority.

Scenario: A teacher wants to move a student to another seat because she is too distracted where she is.

Problem Focus: How to persuade a student to move seat.

Characters: A = Teacher; B = Student.

Role Play

A: Can you just move over to that chair please, Natasha (indicates by pointing at an empty chair at another part of the room).

B: Why have I got to move? I ain't done nothing!

A: I think you'll be more settled over here please, Natasha. Come on! (Teacher moves to the table and takes out the empty chair and holds it in a beckoning way. Then just waits.)

B: No, why don't you move him? Why's it always me?

A: I don't want to argue with you! We must get on with our work. Over here now please! (Teacher stands by the 'destination chair' in a confident way anticipating compliance in the tone of voice and confident body language.)

Natasha does nothing.

A: Natasha, I've asked you several times now. Could you move over here please? (Teacher just waits in a poised way . . . pause) Natasha, I'd like you to move over here please.

B: Oh, you always pick on me (picks up her stuff in a strop and flounces over to the new chair).

The teacher then gets straight on with the lesson.

Points for Reflection and Discussion:

1. Try out the role play again with the teacher changing the pace and severity of the voice and experimenting with the body language. An important thing to experiment with is the length of the pauses.

2. Try moving some of the student's books over to the new seat. Does that work well?

3. What would you do if she still refused to move?

4. The teacher who plays the student can describe how the pressure to move feels with the various ways of doing it.

Scenario: Two students are ignoring the teacher's instructions.

Problem Focus: How to approach a student.

Characters: A: student; B: student; C: teacher.

Role Play

C: Excuse me, you two. I keep asking you to stop chatting and get on with your work please (teacher is by the white board calling over).

A: (ignoring teacher) Did you see that film last night?

B: Yer, it was good. I liked the bit where he jumped off that bridge into that river . . .

C: (moving towards them) I'm sorry, but you have got to stop talking and start some work.

A: Alright, get out of my face will you!

C: (invades the personal space with voice raised) I'm telling you to stop talking and start working!

B: Alright stress head!

C: What did you call me? (getting very angry).

Points for Reflection and Discussion:

Try out this role play a few times and vary the key factors:

1. How quickly the teacher moves towards the students.
2. How strong the teacher's voice is.
3. The teacher's body language.
4. How close to the students does the teacher get?

The teachers who play the part of the students can report how it feels as the teacher gets closer. Which is the most effective distance to keep and tone of voice to use? Experiment with these variables. Moving towards a student does make a powerful point but getting too close can seem threatening. Also try other strategies like where the teacher sits next to the students and redirects attention onto the work. Try it where the teacher starts writing in the student's book and then hands the pen to the student and says 'Come on, let's see what you can do!' and then goes back to the front of the class.

Scenario: A student deliberately misbehaves. When reprimanded, he apologizes and then reverts to another type of low level, but disruptive, behaviour.

Problem Focus: The best way to reprimand.

Characters: A = Teacher; B = Simon, the student who misbehaves; C = a student who comes in from the corridor.

Role Play

A: (from front of the class) I keep telling you, Simon, to stop interrupting. Now you're tapping on the desk.

B: I'm sorry. I won't do it again.

A: Now listen up everyone. This is what I want you to do. Look at chart 1 and then . . . (pause, looks at Simon who has now got ink on his hands and is rubbing it onto his book). Simon, what are you doing now?

B: I'm sorry, my pen's exploded!

A: You're getting the ink everywhere . . . (raising voice) Now get to the toilet and wash your hands! (a period of disruption as Simon leaves the room and quite quickly returns.) Simon, have you washed your hands?

B: No Sir, the toilets was closed. But I've got my hands clean.

A: How did you do that? (Just as Simon begins to explain the door bursts open and a girl charges in and thumps Simon!)

D: That's for wiping your hands on my jacket you creep! (She runs out and of course the class reacts.)

Points for Reflection and Discussion:

1. Repeat the role play again, but this time the teacher quickly sets the class some work and then approaches Simon to re-direct his attention to work.

2. Is it a good idea to let Simon out of the room? Could it have been dealt with keeping him in the room?

3. What are the other types of low level disruptions commonly seen? Is it better to deal with them in front of the class or in a quiet one to one with the student?

BEST WAY TO REPRIMAND

Scenario: You notice that a student is not himself. His behaviour has deteriorated and it is obviously affecting his work. You've decided to have a quiet word after the lesson keeping your teaching assistant with you.

Problem Focus: To try to get to the bottom of a problem with a little chat.

Characters: A = teacher; B = Jake, the student.

Role Play

A: Jake, could I have a quiet word?

B: What's the matter?

A: I've noticed that you're not your normal self lately.

B: What do you mean?

A: Well, if we look at your work compared to a couple of weeks ago it shows that you're not doing much at all. Look at this.

B: I'm tired, that's all. Can I go now?

A: Also, when I look round the room you're often scribbling on Joseph's work.

B: He scribbles on mine!

A: Yes, but the point I'm making Jake, is that you didn't used to be like this. What's wrong?

B: Nothing.

A: Are you sure.

B: I don't want to talk about it.

A: That's fine. I don't want to be nosey, I just want to see if there's anything I, or the school might do to help that's all.

B: (starts crying) I don't understand the work.

A: In this subject?

B: In all subjects. I just don't get it and my dad will kill me if I don't do well (carries on crying).

Points for Reflection and Discussion:

1. The student may be reluctant to open up at first. It is important to judge when to ask other staff for help.

2. What is the best tone and attitude for the teacher to use?

3. Why is it important to have another adult with you?

4. What should be the next step in this situation?

Scenario: A teacher is talking to the whole class.

Problem Focus: How the teacher's reactions create the working atmosphere.

Characters: A = Teacher; B = Megan; C= Grace.

Role Play: Version 1

A: Now listen up class. We are going to be looking at the music of Beethoven today.

B: That's boring! Can't we look at some modern stuff?

A: How dare you call out! We're looking at Beethoven because it's on the syllabus. You sit there calling out all the time. Just listen and try and learn something for once. (long pause, angry stare) Now, as I was saying, we're going to listen to one of Beethoven's Symphonies and . . . .

C: She's right! It's boring rubbish. Put some modern sounds on. Get with it, man!

A: How many times have I told you to shut up? Your modern stuff is rubbish. Beethoven was a genius. Now just listen and don't you dare interrupt me again.

B: Keep your hair on.

C: Take a chill pill mate.

A: Don't you call me mate!

Version 2

A: Now listen up class. We are going to be looking at the music of Beethoven today.

B: That's boring! Can't we look at some modern stuff?

A: (good humoured tone) I suppose you've got a point Megan. It was written a long time ago and may sound a bit strange. I tell you what, give it a go and see what you think.

C: But sir, why can't we listen to modern stuff?

A: The thing is Grace, Beethoven is part of the syllabus. If you listen well perhaps we can pop some of your stuff on at the end. How about that?

C: All right. Stick your Beethoven on. We'll try it . . .

Points for Reflection and Discussion:

Notice how the whole direction of the lesson is governed by the teacher's responses.

YOU'RE PICKING ON ME

Scenario: You have kept back a student for serious misbehaviour and she claims that you are picking on her. Another member of staff is with you.

Problem Focus: How to deal with a student like this.

Characters: A = Teacher; B = Lauren.

Role Play

A: Now Lauren, can we have a quick chat please?

B: I've got nothing to say to you, you pick on me!

A: You threw your work on the floor. You scribbled over the desk. You were uncooperative throughout. We can't go on like this, can we?

B: You don't say nothing to Brooklyn, do yer? She can't do nothing wrong, can she? You pick on me. All the teachers pick on me! (Lauren starts to get angry and upset).

A: (pauses) Lauren, I'm not picking on you, I'm picking on the bad behaviour. You could choose to behave well, couldn't you?

B: I did my work didn't I? Olivia did nothing. You're picking on me and I'm not having it (furious).

A: Lauren, you did do some work, but only in the last few minutes.

B: (Lauren hurls her book across the room and kicks the desks screaming) Well then, I worked and others did nothing! You don't pick on them, do yer? You're a useless teacher.

Points for Reflection and Discussion:

1. Is it a good idea to carry on when the student becomes so angry?

2. What could this seriously develop into?

3. Could the meeting be re-arranged for another time with a senior teacher?

4. Why do you think Lauren is so angry? Is it because she has been tackled and found out?

5. Could Lauren have used this behaviour to scare off teachers in the past?

6. Would finding out what is happening in other subject areas help solve this situation?

Scenario: A student who will not work.

Problem focus: How to persuade a student to work.

Characters: A = Teacher; B = Madeline, the student who won't work.

Role Play: Version 1

A: (moving towards Madeline) Madeline, I've asked you lots of times now to get started with the work.

B: (looks bored) I don't want to do it.

A: We've got to do it. I will not have laziness in my class. (stands over her.) Come on, get on with it.

B: (sniggers to her friend) I don't want to, it's boring.

A: I'm not leaving this spot until you start working.

B: I don't know what to do (still sniggering).

A: But I've explained it clearly! (raises voice) Now get on with it!

Version 2

A: (moving towards Madeline) Are you ok Madeline? Does it all make sense?

B: I don't want to do it.

A: Oh, don't be like that. Let's have a look (sits down next to her). Now look at this (Madeline sniggers to her friend). Come on, Madeline, we must try and concentrate now. You've got to look at the chart and work out where to put that information. Now look, if I do the first one for you will you try the next one? (shows her how and returns the pen) Right, you have a go now and I'll be over to help you in a few moments. Thanks. (Teacher then moves to another student.)

Points for Reflection and Discussion:

1. Which version do you think will produce the best results? Why ?
2. How is the language the teacher uses different in the two versions?
3. What other techniques could the teacher try?
4. Have a go at acting out other ideas which encourage the student to work?

Scenario: Aggression is building between two students.

Problem Focus: How to intervene and deal with such a serious problem.

Characters: A = Teacher; B = Isaac; C = Sean.

Role Play

B: Yer, and you should tell your brother to get stuffed!

C: Tell my brother that and he'd knock you out, mate (body language shows rising aggression).

B: If I phone my uncle he'd be down here now and he'd have the lot of yer (showing rising aggression).

A: Right, that's enough everyone. Let's get back to our work shall we?

C: (totally ignoring teacher) Is that the uncle that Tracy knocked out? (mocking voice . . . starts to rise from seat . . . pre-fight ritual body language begins) He's an idiot mate!

A: I've said that's enough. Sit down the two of you. Now!

B: (anger directed at the teacher) I ain't sitting nowhere. He's got it coming to him (starts moving towards Sean . . . whole class watching and tension rising).

A: (quietly) Amy, could you go to reception and request senior management support immediately please?

Points for Reflection and Discussion

1. At what point should the teacher intervene?
2. Why is it important to have a prearranged contingency plan?
3. What ways are there of getting emergency senior management support?
4. What is the most effective body language and tone of voice for the teacher to use?
5. Where should the teacher stand as the students start to 'face up' to each other?
6. If the students do start fighting what should the teacher do?
7. What should be the minimum arrangements for next lesson?
8. Would the teacher need support in this situation (emotionally)?

Dealing with Extreme Behaviours

Imagine the following situation.

You begin your lesson in the usual way. Maybe there has been a bit of disruption with late comers and a feeling that the class is more unsettled than normal. Something is not quite right. Rose decides to run to the front and make a big thing about putting gum in the bin. Chloe bursts out laughing and a general feeling of unease rapidly develops. Jamie starts to swear openly across at Darren. Peter feels now is the time to throw a pen at Harry. You use your usual techniques to quieten everything down, but something is wrong.

The disruption is spreading and you get that awful feeling of losing control. You sense that they are watching you, waiting for more fun. The odds are stacked in favour of them because there is only one of you and many of them. It is as if strange primordial powers have been aroused and they are ready, as a group, to take you on. Even the usually very well behaved students seem to be strangely poised, watching, ready to join in.

There is only one thing you must do in this situation. That is to call for help. You implement your system of calling out for help immediately. There are some who feel that to call for help is a weakness. The skill of a teacher is to be able to recognize when it is the right time to call for help. To continue with teaching the class in the circumstances described above is not only an error of judgement but it is also dangerous. It is dangerous because it could lead to physical injury in the wake of a kind of anarchy. You will find that such situations are rare compared to the times when you can control things on your own. To call for help in such a situation is not a weakness, but a strength.

Where you have a student who has highly disruptive behaviours I have discovered that 'chunking' can really work wonders.

An illustration:

Gavin calls out repeatedly, when you try to explain something to the class. He then keeps saying sorry and immediately reverts to calling out again. He scribbles on other students' work. He does very little himself. He leaves his seat continuously.

Pick out four behaviours which you want changed. A lot of schools have a formal report system which is very formalized and awkward to manage. This idea involves you and him and your subject, informally and that's all.

You say: 'Look Gavin, you're a likeable lad, you know that. But we can't go on like this, can we? We don't want to go down that route with all that paperwork, phone calls to your parents and all those detentions you would have to do. So I'll tell you what we'll try. Next lesson, I want to see you staying in your seat. That's not too much to ask, is it? Now do we have an agreement?'

The next lesson you particularly look out for him keeping to his word. You are not expecting his extremely poor behaviour to suddenly become perfect, but you are looking for step by step improvements and he's agreed to that. Quietly thank him, at the end and then set another target and so on. As things improve you can offer to send a letter home detailing improvements.

What you manage to achieve with this idea is a sense of progress and a sense of a 'deal' with the student. You've established a sort of order in the chaos. By breaking the big problem into smaller parts it makes the outcome more easily attainable and manageable. You obviously couldn't do this for all students but you can reserve it for severe cases and I have had some fantastic outcomes over the years using this technique.

Sometimes, although you remain friendly and polite to a particular student she has obviously set herself against you. To everything you say, she has a negative response. She tries to get you into an argument. When you gently reprimand her she becomes very defensive. She calls out that the work is too difficult or too easy or she claims that you won't help her. When you do go over and help her with the work she makes silly faces to someone across the room.

The teacher's natural reaction is to reprimand and take the situation up the ladder of consequences. It is a very annoying and undermining set of behaviours.

What should you do? The student is clearly ready to be difficult no matter what you say or do. I think that often there is a lack of self-esteem at issue here.

First, continue to help the student politely, and firmly and politely counter her comments. Keep on with this approach, lesson after lesson, deflecting her comments and behaviour and focusing back to the work. Second, maintain a friendly, firm, caring attitude. Try not to make a big deal of her poor attitude and behaviour. Make comments like, 'Sarah, you really must try to settle down now. You've had loads of time to get started. I do want you to do well.'

After a while you set up a situation where the student starts to believe that you really do care for her well-being, despite how she is treating you. It is a resilience of approach that you need to maintain at all costs. Never resort to anger, because it will never work with a student like this.

Little by little, you will notice that her comments reduce or change. Slowly her behaviour will be more of what is desired. You are investing a gentle, patient and caring approach and you will reap a rich harvest when she decides to put her energies into working rather than opposing you.

LOOK AT ME

As teachers we come across students who command attention using a wide variety of techniques. They may not have learnt much academically during their years at school but they certainly have become expert at commanding attention. They are able to creatively utilize one technique after another and they act as a sort of 'court jester' to the class. They pride themselves on misbehaviour and they are immune to reprimands.

So, faced with such a student, what do you do ? I have found that to confront powerfully this sort of behaviour head on can develop into trouble. I remember a teacher with a zero-tolerance attitude dealing with such a student as described and it really wasn't long before the inevitable happened. Yes, the student was transferred from her class permanently. It solved the problem for that teacher but not for the teacher who inherited that student.

On the other hand, to take a too soft approach, and to pretend that things aren't really too bad, and to conclude that all the student needs is lots of space will lead inevitably to the student effectively taking control of what is happening in your classroom.

So what do you do with such students, and still be able to keep them in your classroom? I have developed a two-layer system. You continue to manage your class using your normal tried and tested methods known as the 'macro system' and at the same time you include a parallel 'micro system' for the student in question.

You keep a closer eye on him and you give feedback when he crosses the line. It is a sort of monitoring process and your comments are fair, firm and well targeted. So really you are allowing him space to 'bubble along a little bit extra' but at the same time managing his behaviour neatly within the context of the whole class.

If you are teaching a student with very demanding behaviour, you can make progress by involving the parent or guardian, not for the purpose of criticism but for the purposes of praise.

A lot of teachers, when I have discussed this idea with them, say things like: 'Bad behaviour is bad behaviour! How can you praise them to their parents?' But it is a fundamental fact of life that the majority of parents see their children as 95 per cent good with only 5 percent room for improvement, however poor their behaviour really is.

The great advantage of this idea is that it gives you a negotiating platform. I'm not suggesting that you have intense and frequent contact with all parents. What you can do is to select those few who give you the biggest worries with behaviour and use this idea for them.

When you discuss matters with the student, before your weekly call, if the behaviour has been utterly appalling, you can negotiate. You can explain that you don't want to phone up and just criticize. You say that nobody wants that. Urge them, cajole them into having some improvement next time and be specific. Then, when the improvement takes place, praise the student and report the improvement back to the parent with a positive sense of progress.

You can, of course, mention the problems which persist, but the point is you do so in the context of how other things are moving slowly in the right direction. It changes the temperature of the discussion and it is much more likely that you will get good support from the parents if you handle it this way.

The power of this idea is that the regular dialogue at home amplifies your own efforts with the student and it has a cumulative effect as time moves on. The parent sees that you are trying to find a ray of light in an otherwise bleak picture.

AGGRESSION TURNED ON YOU

Sometimes, a stressful situation can suddenly escalate and you can find a student is directing her aggression directly at you. There are many reasons why this could suddenly flare up. Maybe you innocently said the wrong thing at the wrong time.

It is obviously a frightening moment and in my whole career it has only happened to me a handful of times. However, it can happen, and I have known of teachers to leave the profession because of it.

So how do you deal with it? I think that every teacher should from time to time practise and rehearse what she would do if such a situation arose. A good way to do it is to arrange with a small group of colleagues to take some time and work through a few role play scenarios where a student turned aggression directly at a teacher. I don't mean actually physical violence, as physical self-defence is a separate, although closely related matter. I refer to the prelude of aggressive comments and threatening body language which can so often lead on to physical violence.

Learn how to use your voice and body language and poise and hand gestures to firmly and calmly de-escalate the situation. Practise it with your colleagues; you will find it extremely useful. In fact, it is only through practise that you learn effective techniques to calm such situations. You have to pitch it right. If you act submissively that can often encourage an assault. Be too firm and that too can cause an escalation.

Clearly every situation is different and of course you never know how things will develop. But in order to stack the probability of a satisfactory outcome in your favour, prior practise and training is a must. Hopefully, you will never need to use it, but the training will give you that important edge and help you take control if such a situation did flare up.

If you have a situation where, despite the use of your best techniques, the class is still misbehaving taking you to the edge of your ability to control, then what do you do?

An instinctive reaction is for the teacher to shout. Unfortunately, that technique is doomed to failure. The class would probably regard the teacher's behaviour as entertaining and laugh at it! At best the technique might subdue the class for a short while but the behaviour would soon deteriorate again.

Of course the most popular option, in this situation, is to call for senior teacher assistance. That's fine but there is something you could try before calling for help.

Stand calmly at the front of the class with the usual posture of quiet assertive presence. Then ask quietly, firmly and repeatedly for them to stop what they are doing, put their pens down and fold their arms.

If you confidently repeat the instructions you will be surprised how many comply. You wait. You repeat the instructions. Your expression has a firmness of determination about it.

Then, when the vast majority are listening you say: 'I have tried all the normal ways to encourage you to work and clearly, for some reason today, a great many of you have decided to totally ignore my instructions. This is very serious. I now have no choice but to write a full report to the head teacher to explain why I have had to suspend this lesson.'

You wait and start writing the report. You then say: 'Obviously, if you quietly start working from now on your name will not be included in the report. I realize that it isn't the whole class ignoring me!' You carry on writing the report.

You will be surprised how many students will start quietly working, as the majority will not want to get into trouble. You will find that this technique restores back to you the balance of power and will enable you to continue the lesson.

GANGING UP ON YOU

One extreme behaviour which is very difficult to deal with is when a group of students, in the classroom, deliberately gang up against you.

Characteristic of this behaviour is that one of the group defiantly misbehaves and, when you challenge the behaviour, other members of the group spring to their defence. Others join in when you become firmer in response and you get the impression that you are taking on the whole class.

You will also find that they are highly skilled at their ganging up routine because they often have had a lot of practise with other teachers and have seen how effective it is in unnerving them.

The effect can be devastating to the teacher. If it is clear that you are experiencing a sustained and continuing ganging up scenario against you, then you must involve senior colleagues. You do need to do a bit of research to establish whether this behaviour is affecting other lessons. You also need to collect a lot of evidence to be sure about what is going on. However, this is a very serious situation and no teacher should be left to try to deal with it on their own.

Once it is firmly established that a ganging up situation is taking place against you, then you must arrange immediately to have the members of the group permanently transferred into different classes under the 'divide and conquer' rule.

Sometimes, despite the use of tried and tested behaviour management strategies a student may be completely defiant. It can take an endless variety of forms. Take for example, a student who is on her mobile phone texting away, and you ask her to put the phone away and she replies: 'No, get out of my face!' and sounds quite aggressive. You give her space and go through the usual recommended ways of encouraging her to comply. But she does not comply. She defiantly carries on with what she is doing and your authority over the situation seems to have disappeared.

In many cases of classroom misbehaviour the situation can be skilfully defused by deferring dealing with it until later, or at the end of the lesson, to allow you to keep the momentum of the lesson going forward. However, if you deferred a case such as this, of outright defiance and said that you will speak to her at the end of the lesson, you give a clear message to the rest of the class that outright defiance works. The problem you would then have is getting others to comply because for lesser misdemeanours they would simply say: 'But Chloe can do what she likes, why can't I?' This situation will seriously weaken your authority.

Part of the skill of a teacher is to know when to react and at what level to react at. In the case of blatant defiance, I think you will find it to be mercifully rare that it does not respond, or partially respond, to your normal techniques. In this example, however, I think it is always best to have the student swiftly removed from your lesson so that you can continue with your lesson and deal with the student later. You will need to get to the root of this behaviour before she can be readmitted into your class.

THE BOTTOM LINE

A lot of behaviour advice refers to the importance of inclusion and the need for endless care and patience with students who have challenging behaviour.

Some teachers take the strong, opposing and understandable view that a student who continually and wilfully misbehaves has no right to mess up the learning of all the others in the group.

I also have seen teachers make so many allowances for their challenging students, that they have forgotten about the other students, who do not misbehave and who are losing out.

My own solution in getting the balance right is to use all the strategies I can to include difficult students. I try to be like a referee who does not pick up every little thing and therefore allows the game to flow.

But I do have a bottom line and my students know it. There are times when despite all my fair and professional approach, a student disregards it all and does whatever he wants. This is where I bring in a senior member of staff for an after the lesson special meeting. I explain very clearly everything I have done and show how reasonable it all is. Then I set next to that the behaviours of the student which are so obviously totally unacceptable.

There may well be an endless list of home circumstances which have caused this student to be so difficult. There may well be. But in practice, when I set out so clearly why I am so annoyed (and I do show annoyance without showing anger) that my bottom line has been crossed, then almost always the student changes their behaviour for the better.

They see that you have been reasonable and they also see that they have gone too far. They see that they have crossed your bottom line.

So with extremely challenging students do all you can to be reasonable, but leave them in no doubt as to where your bottom line is!

A Few 'Off the Wall' Strategies

It takes courage and experience to actually say to the class, 'maybe I was partly to blame' but I have found this to be a very powerful tool, if used correctly.

If you have carefully analysed what happened after a particularly bad lesson you may well find a combination of their poor behaviour and maybe work which was not as well prepared or suitable as it could have been. Be careful only to use this technique sparingly and with classes you know well.

Begin the lesson by outlining what went wrong in the last lesson. Explain that you realize that while their behaviour was not good, that was not the whole explanation as to why things went wrong.

You may, for example say: 'I've looked again at the work I'd prepared for you and I think, perhaps, it was a little too difficult, maybe a bit confusing!' Then explain what you have done to put things right. Explain that you have perhaps re-written the worksheets and included extra help sheets. Importantly explain that you are going to try the lesson again. Say something like: 'Now that I've got the work better for you and with your improved behaviour, together I'm sure we can have a much better lesson today, don't you? Come on let's have a good lesson!'

The students will see that you are being fair and that you have taken the time and trouble to reflect on exactly what went wrong. They will see you as a conscientious professional and someone who is not too proud or aloof to take a proportion of the blame. All this works together to persuade them to behave better and you will find that, if used cautiously, this technique will make the behaviour much better. It also helps in the long term to build integrity and engender strong teacher-student relationships.

THE INDIVIDUAL PRIVATE TRACK RECORD

People like to know that they are building up a good track record but what about students with low self-esteem, poor results and challenging behaviour? If you were to display their academic results to the class, you would regret it. You could find that you are reinforcing and broadcasting their sense of failure.

I have found a way, with challenging classes, to harness the power of the pride taken in a track record without the risk of negative responses. I call it 'The Individual Private Track Record'. It is a simple system. You keep a special book listing your students' names and you enter notes, comments and responses to various aspects of their work. The focus of the things you select to record are aspects which you can attach positive improvements to (however slight the improvements may be).

The best way to use the book is to show them their page when you can have a short private word with them or after the lesson. It is important to keep a completely separate page for each student.

The value of this idea is that it shows the student that you care and that you are actively looking for good things to write in the book. The key is to actively and continually, look out for tiny improvements in a whole range of areas. Examples of notes you may include are:

> 'Daniel entered the room with a more settled behaviour than last lesson.'
> 'Rachel scribbled far less in her exercise book today.'
> 'Charlie called out far less than last lesson and put his hand up a few times.'

Your attitude has to be sincere with the students and they have to believe and trust that you are genuinely pleased about the small improvements. If that happens, and it will, if you use meticulous persistence, then you will find that such a record will, over time, help to gradually bring their behaviour round to be closer to your expectations.

You are approaching the end of the lesson and the noise levels are rising. The energy of the class means that your voice alone is failing dismally at controlling them at this stage. You try other noise control techniques but the raw energy of the class is too much for them. So what do you do?

Try this. As an introduction to the plenary at the end, you prominently write out two teams 'A' and 'B' on the board and say these words: 'Bonus point to the quietest side!' and you stand poised with your pen.

Now, it is vital that you do not write anything yet. The noise level will fall and for a while may become silent, as you decide. Now try this. You say these words: 'As you are both quiet, I can't decide which team is best. I'll have to use the "no fidget rule". Now you know how this works. We need to see who can have absolutely no fidgets at all for the longest? I'll warn you, it's not easy . . . you're not even allowed to scratch your head! Not every class can do this . . .'

Now you hold this, looking at your watch. You will be amazed at how long you can hold the class silent with this technique. I don't know why it works so well. Maybe it brings out the power of games children play when they are very small. The beauty is that it allows all the noise energy to be focused into silent energy. Say things like 'marvellous, well done' as you hold the silence. Be sure to say: 'Not long now . . .' as you look at your watch. Then award the points to the winner (say it was hard to choose!)

You will them have them quiet enough to start the plenary. Don't forget, if the noise rises up again, simply use the technique again (but don't overdo it).

HOW DO YOU DESCRIBE THINGS?

Students react to certain words and phrases in a predictable way. Words are loaded with emotion and feelings. If you say, for example 'come into the classroom', the word 'classroom' has negative connotations and lowers the mood, subconsciously. If, instead you say: 'Enter this temple of learning!' you create a more positive feel to what is happening. Don't refer to exercise books by that boring name, call them 'records of great thoughts and experiments'.

Don't ever say the word 'test' as it creates unhappy mental pictures. Say that 'we now have a great opportunity to show what we have remembered!'

Don't say I want to tell you a 'story' as that word can curiously be negative for many. Instead say ' a set of exciting events'.

The more you think about it and experiment with what you call things, the more you can bring things alive and add interest. Even something like: 'I'm going to show you a picture' can have a bland and dull feel to it, because of familiarity with so many pictures in so many lessons. Instead say: 'In a moment I'm going to show you something that for millions of years mankind never, ever saw !' Then show them a picture of the earth seen from space.

I'm sure you can develop your own positive language when you name things. If you are cheerful and positive this idea introduces a bit more fun into the proceedings. Sometimes there are negative comments from students but they soon get used to it and in fact many start using your terms and then you know things are going really well.

I didn't realize quite how effective this idea was until I was away from one of my own lessons once and a cover teacher told me that at 10 minutes before the end the students started to demand their 'world famous plenary!' They apparently said: 'Oh, we always have a world famous plenary at the end of the lesson!'

It is my experience that if you speak to the average teacher, the chances are that they will be 'wound up' by something. Teaching is a high risk profession for stress and the wind ups come from a huge variety of sources. Maybe a student has been particularly obnoxious; maybe the lessons they spent hours preparing were chucked onto the floor; maybe a harassed colleague has been off hand . . . the possibilities are endless.

Feeling wound up puts a huge drag on your energies when faced with students with challenging behaviour. I have discovered a simple but highly effective technique for counterbalancing your reactions to being wound up. Expect it ! It is as simple as that. Also, don't just expect it but maintain a pocket notebook where you record your daily windups. Obviously only put the really bad ones, rather than all the little things. On each page number one to seven and as the wind ups come in, jot them down against the number. It turns the whole situation into a kind of game. You may think, 'I've had a good day today, look only five wind ups instead of the usual seven!'

By having an attitude of anticipation for daily wind ups you will find that they no longer have the power to drag down your mood in quite the same way as before. You realize very clearly that you are in a high pressure environment and being would up is an unavoidable part of the whole picture.

As time goes by your wind up book becomes even more effective because you can look back and see the truth that they will always happen. It is not the fact that they happen which is the problem but your reaction to it. I recommend that every teacher maintain a wind up book which, if used everyday will counterbalance the situation, foster peace of mind and help you tackle poor behaviour with a better frame of mind.

THE LITTLE ONE TO ONE SESSIONS

You find that some students with constantly silly behaviour can be very wearing to a teacher. The usual channels are followed with reports and referrals and all the usual sanctions but you find that none of them work. The student may well keep repeating that he is sorry and the behaviour may even improve in a temporary way. The point is that the basic behaviour remains frustratingly poor.

A highly effective way to tackle this is with a technique known as a 'little one to one'. You arrange to see the student on a very regular basis, after the lesson if possible, or at lunch time or after school. The sessions will be quite short. During these sessions you repeat a process. That is, you go through briefly what the inappropriate behaviour was, you explain very clearly why it concerns you and you ask the student how the situation could be resolved. You put the onus back on the student. An important point is to remain cheerful and upbeat and show that you are genuinely interested as to why the behaviour still hasn't improved. You show genuine concern and interest in the student. You suggest in a friendly encouraging way one or two things he might try.

The basic fact is that if you keep following this up the student eventually gets totally fed up with the sessions. I have found that in most cases the behaviour improves dramatically because they just can't face the tedium of going through any more 'little one to ones'!

If you see poor behaviour from that student in the class you just, in a matter of fact way, say 'We'll sort this out in the next little one to one session! OK?' Then you move onto the next student. You give the overwhelming impression that, far from being annoyed, you actually look forward to the sessions to try to help the student get to the heart of why things are going wrong.

THE SECRET CODE

I came upon this idea by sheer chance one day. I don't know why it works quite so well but I do know that it does work if used cautiously when all else seems not to work.

If you are experiencing a particularly difficult time with a student with challenging behaviour and they are being very negative about the work and nothing you say will persuade them to do it, then try to build into your conversation a 'secret code'.

The way you construct this is to build up, over time, a knowledge of what students really love and have passion for. It is amazing what they will tell you in casual conversation. Jot down notes about it because that information will become very useful. The best way to show how this works is to give an example.

Supposing that Brett is pushing his work in technology to one side. He can't see the point and he's in a bad and negative mood. You want him to design a new type of chair, for example, and he just won't co-operate. He can't see the point and he's got himself into a bad mood.

Now, you happen to know that he has a passion for, shall we say, the pop star Katy Perry. You then get him to visualize a connection between Katy Perry and the chair he has to design. Maybe he has won a competition to design a chair especially for her. Now, what would that chair look like ? By involving his passion into the mix, it acts like a secret code and you will find that can often be the tipping point required to get your students to work well.

With creative imagination you will be surprised how well you can make a meaningful and interesting connection between students' particular passions and interests and the work waiting to be done.

THE MUSIC CUE

To get the students to listen at the beginning of a lesson and also during the lesson, at key points I use a music cue. I have a CD Player on the ready and play a few seconds of music quite loud. I then slowly turn the volume down and say: 'That, is better than shouting!' I then go straight into what I want to say.

If you find that after the music cue some are still talking, then say: 'Oh dear! Most people responded beautifully to the music cue. Just a few more now. Let's have another go at this now. One more time and . . .' Play the music again and then pause it and you will find that it works beautifully.

As a teacher you are not just teaching your subject. You are teaching your students how to be good citizens. When it comes to life skills, I look for examples of inappropriate behaviour and then sometimes use them as triggers to demonstrate something by use of an anecdotal story. These eccentric little parables are very popular with my students and I am often asked to repeat them. They are very helpful for making it clear as to why good behaviour is so important.

For example, often a student will have no patience at all. Perhaps she is asking for her exercise book and as you look for it she demands it immediately. She huffs and puffs if she can't have it immediately. I tell her about the rich man in the posh hotel who rang room service and asked for caviar and champagne to be brought to his room now. The waiter said that he would bring it up straight away. The man said: 'You don't understand me, I said I want it now!' Then I say to the student: 'You don't want to end up being like that do you? Come on, you're a nice person, have a bit of patience.'

With experience you can build up a surprisingly large range of stories and fables to match all sorts of bad behaviour. I use them as an entertaining and light-hearted way of making a serious point.

If you are brave enough to do silly voices and actions, then it seems to make them even more effective. It's a way of separating the behaviour from the student and showing why that behaviour is not suitable for that student.

I have used this idea for many years and it has become one of the most popular things I do. It is a kind of 'reward' at the end of the lesson, if the students achieve enough and behave well. It is something different from the lesson and therefore gives their minds a welcome rest. It is eclectic and fun. Over the years I have kept developing what I do in this session and I mention here just a few examples to give an indication of how it works. When everything is done and cleared away and the class is all set to finish the lesson we have our 'Something Completely Different Spot'.

I might show them an optical illusion (projected to the screen) or an extreme close up of an everyday object and they have to guess what it is. I might tell them about an amazing fact for example, Vincent Van Gogh died in poverty but his paintings sell for millons. (Show them a few examples).

I might tell them a short funny story or a heart-warming tale. The students might contribute with very short stories of their own. I have had students come to the front to show me a new dance they've learnt or perhaps sing a song or bring something interesting in from home. There are so many things which you could include. Students love it. One of things they love is the eclectic and unpredictable nature of the session. While short and snappy, these sessions work well and can be included at the end of all the lessons if you want to.

It is another technique that you can use to help encourage good behaviour because you can say things like: 'Oh dear, we're not making the progress we should. At this rate we won't be able to fit in the "Something Completely Different Spot!"'. You will be amazed at how the students respond so positively to that.